SHARED HISTORIES: COMPARING JEWISH AND AFRICAN DIASPORAS

SHADOWS OF SUFFERING:

A COMPARATIVE HISTORY OF THE JEWISH AND AFRICAN DIASPORAS

YEMI ADESINA

APOLOGIA

There are bound to be – only a few, I hope – errors and omissions, and I apologise in advance. No man knows it all, especially me! And you learn more as you get older. One good thing that comes with age is that you are happy to confess what you don't know and pass the inquiry on to a specialist who probably does.

This book is dedicated to hardworking, patient, enthusiastic, generally under-rewarded, and underappreciated people of Africa, those at home and in the diaspora, and everyone interested in the welfare of the continent of Africa.

CONTENTS

ACKNOWLEDGMENTS

While one individual's name may grace the cover of this book, its creation and completion are the result of a collective effort, an alliance of minds and spirits dedicated to the exploration of knowledge and understanding. To each and every one who contributed, directly or indirectly, I extend my heartfelt gratitude.

First and foremost, I acknowledge the divine presence of God Almighty. His boundless grace and guidance have been my steadfast companions throughout this research journey, enabling me to transform ideas into words and thoughts into chapters.

To my late father, Mr. Solomon Olajide Adesina, whose wisdom and encouragement were my pillars of strength, I offer my deepest appreciation. Your memory lives on within these pages.

To my beloved wife, Bola, whose unwavering love, and support have made this venture possible, I owe immeasurable thanks. Your patience and understanding allowed me to embark on countless journeys, to delve into extensive research, and to immerse myself in African history with vigour.

My two sons, Femi and Seun, represent the vibrant second-generation African diaspora in the United Kingdom. Their invaluable insights, engaging discussions, and the spirited debates that often stretched into the late hours have enriched this book immeasurably. I have immense faith in their generation's capacity to shape Africa's future, and I am grateful for their contributions.

My journey of discovery was guided by the wisdom of exceptional individuals who shared their knowledge and insights. Among them, I draw inspiration from the teachings of Pastor Matthew Ashimolowo, the late Dr. Myles Munroe, Dr. Mensah Otabil, and Bishop Tudor Bismark. These spiritual leaders devoted their time and energy to the belief that Africa possesses the potential for great transformation.

A debt of gratitude is owed to Dr. Howard Nicholas, the distinguished economist and researcher from Erasmus University Rotterdam, and Patrick Manning, Jeffrey D. Sachs and his colleagues, whose work on geography's impact resonated deeply with the themes explored in this book. The writings of Walter Rodney, particularly "How Europe Underdeveloped Africa," proved to be an invaluable resource.

I wish to express my appreciation to Britanica.com and Yemi Adeyemi, the visionary founder of ThinkAfrica.net, for their contributions to the discourse on Africa's development.

This book would not be complete without acknowledging the vast community of Jewish and African scholars, experts, and everyday citizens who have enriched the body of knowledge that informs its content. The voices of the Jews and Africa are many, diverse, and resonant, and it has been a privilege to amplify some of them. I encourage readers to continue exploring, to seek out additional perspectives, and to engage in the ongoing dialogue that shapes Africa's narrative.

In closing, I offer my deepest thanks to everyone, organization, and source that has played a part in the creation of this work. Your collective influence has been instrumental in bringing "Shadows of Suffering: A Comparative History of the Jewish and African Diasporas" to life.

BOOK BACK COVER

Mr. Yemi Adesina is a visionary on a mission to transform Africa. With a rich blend of expertise in social work, farming, and African history, Mr. Yemi is a multifaceted leader dedicated to driving positive change across the continent.

As the CEO of Pristine Integrated Farm Resources Ltd, a non-profit organization, he is committed to promoting youth and rural empowerment, alleviating poverty through education in Africa. Mr. Yemi's written works are a testament to his deep under-standing of Africa's challenges and potential. From "Why Africa Cannot Feed Itself and the Way Forward" to "Does the World Need Africa," his books tackle critical issues facing the continent with a forward-thinking perspective.

After two decades of academic and professional growth in the United Kingdom, he made the life-changing decision to return to Nigeria in 2010.

In this book, we looked at the complex tapestry of human history, there are threads of suffering that stretch across continents and centuries. "Shadows of Suffering: " is a profound exploration of two such threads—the Jewish and African diasporas.

What makes "Shadows of Suffering" particularly remarkable is its dedication to comparative history. By juxtaposing the experiences of Jewish and African diasporas, it seeks to unveil the common threads that bind their stories. Through this comparative lens, we gain a deeper understanding of the universal themes of loss, endurance, and the relentless pursuit of freedom and justice.

The author of this book has undertaken a monumental task—to bridge gaps in our understanding and empathy. He challenges us to acknowledge the shared struggles of these two communities while respecting the uniqueness of their experiences. It is through this delicate balance that we find a path to unity and solidarity.

THE AUTHOR

Mr. Yemi Adesina is not your average author; he is a visionary on a mission to transform Africa. With a rich blend of expertise in social work, farming, and African history, Mr. Yemi is a multifaceted leader dedicated to driving positive change across the continent.

As the CEO of Pristine Integrated Farm Resources Ltd, a non-profit organization, Mr. Yemi is committed to promoting youth and rural empowerment, alleviating poverty through education, and elevating subsistence farming to thriving commercial enterprises in Africa. His passion for sustainable agriculture is evident in his comprehensive guide, "Profitable Pig Farming: A Step-by-Step Guide to Commercial Pig Farming from an African Perspective," which offers valuable insights into the agricultural landscape.

Not only does Mr. Yemi excel as a farmer and advocate for rural development, but he is also a prolific trainer. His YouTube channel, "papayemo1," boasts a collection of 150 videos covering farming techniques and African history. With over 2.5 million viewers from more than 36 countries, his channel stands as a testament to his dedication to sharing knowledge and empowering individuals across the globe.

Mr. Yemi's written works are a testament to his deep understanding of Africa's challenges and potential. From "Why Africa Cannot Feed Itself and the Way Forward" to "Does the World Need Africa," his books tackle critical issues facing the continent with a forward-thinking perspective.

Having emigrated to the United Kingdom in 1991, Mr. Yemi pursued two master's degrees, one in business administration and another in social work. After two decades of academic and professional growth, he made the life-changing decision to return to Nigeria in 2010. His goal was clear: to contribute significantly to Africa's food production and drive positive change in his homeland.

In essence, Mr. Yemi Adesina embodies the spirit of diaspora return, armed with expertise, passion, and an unwavering commitment to Africa's progress. His journey from the United Kingdom to Nigeria is a testament to his dedication to making a meaningful impact.

Through his diverse experiences, comprehensive knowledge, and boundless enthusiasm, Mr. Yemi Adesina is not just an author but a catalyst for change. His work bridges the worlds of agriculture, history, and social progress, offering a beacon of hope and inspiration for the continent he calls home.

FOREWORD

In the complex tapestry of human history, there are threads of suffering that stretch across continents and centuries. "Shadows of Suffering: A Comparative History of the Jewish and African Diasporas" is a profound exploration of two such threads—the Jewish and African diasporas. Through meticulous research, insightful analysis, and a commitment to unveiling the shared experiences of these two communities, this book offers a compelling narrative that illuminates the past and mirrors our present and future.

Though distinct in origin, the Jewish and African diasporas have been bound together by the weight of displacement, discrimination, and the enduring quest for identity and belonging. As we journey through the pages of this book, we are invited to witness the resilience and fortitude of these communities in the face of unimaginable hardships.

Its dedication to comparative history makes "Shadows of Suffering" particularly remarkable. By juxtaposing the experiences of Jewish and African diasporas, it seeks to unveil the common threads that bind their stories. Through this comparative lens, we understand the universal themes of loss, endurance, and the relentless pursuit of freedom and justice.

The author of this book has undertaken a monumental task—to bridge gaps in our understanding and empathy. He challenges us to acknowledge the shared struggles of these two communities while respecting the uniqueness of their experiences. Through this delicate balance, we find a path to unity and solidarity.

In a world where division and prejudice persist, "Shadows of Suffering" symbolises hope and enlightenment. It calls upon us to recognise the shared humanity transcending cultural, religious, and geographical boundaries. It reminds us that by studying the shadows of suffering, we can discover the enduring light of resilience, hope, and unity.

As we embark on this enlightening journey, may we approach it with an open heart and a commitment to learning from the past? Let's draw inspiration from the stories within these pages to work toward a future where suffering is lessened and compassion reigns supreme.

This book is an invaluable contribution to the annals of history and a testament to the indomitable human spirit. It is my privilege to introduce "Shadows of Suffering: A Comparative History of the Jewish and African Diasporas" to you, the reader. May it inspire reflection, dialogue, and, ultimately, positive change.

CHAPTER 1
THE RELEVANCE OF "SHADOWS OF SUFFERING"

THE BOOK "SHADOWS OF SUFFERING: A Comparative History of the Jewish and African Diasporas" holds immense importance in a world marked by increasing globalisation, interconnectedness, and ongoing struggles for justice and equality. This chapter explores why this comparative history is academically valuable and critically relevant in today's context.

Understanding Historical Injustices: One of the primary reasons this book is crucial today is its capacity to shed light on the historical injustices endured by Jewish and African diaspora communities. By delving into the experiences of these two groups, the book provides a nuanced understanding of the complex legacies of slavery, colonisation, and persecution. This historical context is vital for recognising and addressing contemporary issues related to discrimination, racism, and inequality.

Highlighting the Universality of Injustice: "Shadows of Suffering" serves as a reminder of the universality of injustice and suffering. By comparing the experiences of two distinct communities, the book emphasises that suffering transcends cultural, religious, and geographical boundaries. This universal aspect of suffering underscores the importance of solidarity and collective efforts in combating discrimination and oppression worldwide.

Promoting Empathy and Compassion: The book's exploration of the emotional and human dimensions of suffering fosters empathy and compassion among its readers. It encourages individuals to place themselves in the shoes of those who have experienced discrimination and marginalisation, fostering a greater understanding of the lasting impact of historical injustices on communities and individuals.

Encouraging Dialogue and Collaboration: "Shadows of Suffering" offers a platform for dialogue and collaboration between communities, scholars, and activists. It encourages open discussions about historical injustices, their contemporary implications, and ways to address them. The comparative approach invites diverse voices to come together, share their experiences, and work collectively toward a more just and equitable world.

Acknowledging the Universal Nature of Displacement: The Jewish and African diasporas exemplify the universal nature of displacement. They teach us that migration and forced exile are not isolated events but part of a broader human experience. Recognising this universality encourages us to approach contemporary migration with empathy and compassion. It reminds us that regardless of background, displacement can happen to anyone.

Providing Safe Havens and Asylum: Both diasporas have experienced the dire consequences of being denied safe havens and asylum. The tragic consequences of such denial are evident in events like the Holocaust and the horrors of the transatlantic slave trade. Learning from these historical tragedies, we must advocate for robust asylum systems prioritising human rights and providing refuge to those fleeing violence, persecution, and natural disasters.

Addressing Root Causes: The historical narratives in this book highlight the importance of addressing root causes of displacement, whether religious persecution, political instability, or economic hardships. Our approach to contemporary migration and refugee issues must extend beyond humanitarian aid to address the systemic causes of displacement. This involves diplomacy, conflict resolution, and efforts to reduce poverty and inequality.

Inspiring Social Change: The book serves as an inspiration for social change and activism. By highlighting Jewish and African diaspora communities' resilience, resistance, and triumphs it motivates individuals and communities to confront and challenge systemic inequalities and discrimination. It showcases the power of collective action and advocacy.

Fostering Cultural Understanding: "Shadows of Suffering" deepens cultural understanding by showcasing the rich histories, traditions, and values of both Jewish and African diaspora communities. It promotes cultural exchange and appreciation and fosters an environment of mutual respect and cross-cultural dialogue.

The Role of Education and Awareness: Education is a powerful tool for creating awareness about historical injustices and fostering a sense of responsibility to address them. "Shadows of Suffering" serves as an educational resource that can be integrated into academic curricula, promoting discussions about the comparative history of the Jewish and African diasporas. Through educational initiatives, this book can contribute to raising a generation of individuals who are well-informed about the historical struggles of marginalised communities and are motivated to work toward a more just world.

Empowering Activists and Advocates: For activists and advocates engaged in social justice movements, "Shadows of Suffering" offers valuable insights into the strategies and tactics the Jewish and African diaspora communities employ to combat discrimination and oppression. By studying these communities' historical experiences and successes, contemporary activists can draw inspiration and guidance for their advocacy work.

Contributing to Healing and Reconciliation: "Shadows of Suffering" contributes to healing and reconciliation efforts. By acknowledging past injustices, communities can begin the process of reconciliation and healing. This book can catalyse conversations within communities and between different groups, fostering understanding and empathy.

"Shadows of Suffering: A Comparative History of the Jewish and African Diasporas" is a vital resource for our time, offering insights into the enduring legacies of historical injustices and their relevance to contemporary struggles for justice, equality, and cultural preservation. Its impact goes beyond academia, extending to education, activism, advocacy, and global dialogue. By engaging with this book, individuals and communities can gain a deeper understanding of the complexities of history and work collectively to create a more inclusive, compassionate, and just world for all.

In a world where the shadows of historical suffering continue to cast their influence on contemporary societies, "Shadows of Suffering: A Comparative History of the Jewish and African Diasporas" is a beacon of knowledge, empathy, and hope. It reminds us that the struggles of the past shape our present and that learning from history is essential to building a more inclusive, compassionate, and just world. This book is a testament to the enduring legacies of resilience and the human spirit's capacity to overcome adversity. Its relevance lies in understanding the past and inspiring meaningful action in the present and future.

CHAPTER 2
INTRODUCTION TO THE DIASPORA CONCEPT

THE CONCEPT of the diaspora is a complex and multifaceted idea that has significantly shaped the history, culture, and identities of various communities worldwide. Derived from the Greek word "diaspeirein," which means "to scatter" or "to disperse," the term "diaspora" refers to the dispersion or scattering of a group of people from their ancestral homeland to different regions or countries. The concept of the diaspora is often used to describe the experiences of communities that have faced forced or voluntary migration, exile, or displacement.

Diasporas have been a common phenomenon in human history, dating back to ancient times. Various factors, including conflict, persecution, economic opportunity, trade, and colonisation, have driven them. The Jewish diaspora, for example, is one of the most well-known and historically significant diasporas, with Jewish communities scattered across the globe.

What distinguishes diaspora communities is their unique position as both insiders and outsiders in their host societies. They maintain strong connections to their ancestral homeland while adapting to their new environments' cultures, languages, and social structures. This dual identity often creates distinctive cultural expressions, hybrid identities, and a sense of belonging to multiple places.

Key characteristics and aspects of the diaspora concept include:

Diversity: Diaspora communities are incredibly diverse, reflecting various ethnic, religious, linguistic, and cultural backgrounds. This diversity is often a source of strength and resilience for these communities.

Cultural Preservation: Diaspora communities frequently engage in efforts to preserve and transmit their cultural heritage, including language, traditions, cuisine, and religious practices. These cultural elements can evolve and adapt in the diaspora context.

Identity and Belonging: Diaspora communities grapple with questions of identity and belonging. They often maintain strong emotional ties to their ancestral homeland while forging new identities as members of their host societies.

Transnationalism: Diaspora communities often engage in transnational activities, such as remittances, trade, and political activism, that bridge their homeland and host country. This transnational engagement can have significant economic and political implications.

Challenges and Opportunities: Diaspora communities face various challenges, including discrimination, assimilation pressures, and the longing for their homeland. At the same time, they contribute to their host societies' diversity and cultural richness and can play a role in diplomacy and international relations.

Historical and Contemporary Significance: Diasporas have played pivotal roles in historical events, such as the Jewish and African diasporas. In the contemporary world, diaspora communities continue to have a global social and economic impact.

Understanding the concept of the diaspora is essential for comprehending the complexities of global migration, cultural exchange, and the interconnectedness of societies. It sheds light on the resilience and adaptability of human communities in the face of displacement and change. Throughout history, diaspora communities have contributed significantly to their host countries' cultural, economic, and political landscapes and the world at large.

CHAPTER 3
SIMILARITIES IN INJUSTICE: JEWS AND BLACK AFRICANS

THROUGHOUT HUMAN HISTORY, the world has witnessed the plight of diverse communities subjected to persecution, discrimination, and displacement. Among these communities, the Jewish and African peoples stand out as two groups whose histories are marked by profound struggles and enduring resilience. "Shadows of Suffering" is a comprehensive exploration of the shared and contrasting experiences of Jews and Black Africans during their diasporic journeys.

Historically, it was not until the 18th century, with the rise of Old Testament–oriented Protestantism among blacks under slavery in North America and the growing awareness of injustice and marginalisation among Jews, that the blacks and Jews began to sense some similarities between their two histories.

Historical Roots of Persecution: Both Jews and Black Africans have faced persecution rooted in deeply ingrained biases. Jews have faced anti-Semitism, which has historical and religious origins, while Black Africans have endured racism based on the notion of racial superiority and inferiority.

Expulsions and Displacement: Both groups have experienced forced expulsions and displacement. Jews were expelled from various European countries during the Middle Ages, while Black Africans were forcibly displaced through the transatlantic slave trade and colonialism.

Discriminatory Laws and Practices: Discriminatory laws and practices have been employed against both communities. Jews faced restrictions on property ownership, employment, and participation in public life in Europe. Similarly, Black Africans faced legal discrimination under Jim Crow laws in the United States, apartheid in South Africa, and colonial segregation in Africa.

Stereotyping and Dehumanization: Stereotyping and dehumanization have been used against Jews and Black Africans. Jews were often depicted as greedy, conniving, and responsible for societal ills, while Black Africans were dehumanized through derogatory stereotypes and racial caricatures.

Economic Exploitation: Both groups were subjected to economic exploitation. Jews were often targeted for their economic success and faced economic restrictions. Black Africans were enslaved and forced to labour in inhumane conditions, contributing significantly to the wealth of European and American societies.

Violent Pogroms and Lynchings: Violent pogroms against Jewish communities and lynchings of Black individuals are disturbing similarities in their histories. Both groups faced mob violence and were targeted for their perceived differences.

Resilience and Resistance: Jews and Black Africans have demonstrated resilience and resistance throughout their histories. Both have formed underground movements, engaged in protests, and fought for their rights and dignity in the face of systemic oppression.

Diaspora and Cultural Preservation: Despite dispersion and oppression, both communities have preserved their cultures, traditions, and identities in the diaspora. Jewish communities maintained their religious practices and language, while Black Africans preserved their cultural elements through music, art, and oral traditions.

Pursuit of Equality and Justice: Both Jews and Black Africans have been at the forefront of civil rights and social justice movements. Jewish activists have fought against anti-Semitism and for human rights, while Black activists have led movements against racial discrimination and for equality.

Ongoing Challenges: Both groups continue to face challenges related to discrimination and marginalization in contemporary societies. Jews and Black Africans are still affected by discrimination, racism, and prejudice in various forms.

Religious Discrimination: Both groups faced religious discrimination. Jews faced religious persecution based on their beliefs, including forced conversions and religious restrictions. Black Africans experienced religious suppression through the imposition of Christianity during the era of colonization.

Impact on Cultural Identity: Marginalization has had a profound impact on the cultural identities of both communities. Jews in the diaspora have maintained a strong cultural and religious identity despite centuries of persecution. Similarly, Black Africans in the diaspora have preserved their cultural elements, including language, music, and spirituality, as a means of resisting erasure.

Disproportionate Suffering: Both Jews and Black Africans have experienced disproportionate suffering compared to other groups. Jews endured the Holocaust, a genocidal event, while Black Africans endured the horrors of the transatlantic slave trade, which led to unimaginable suffering and loss of life.

Struggles for Recognition: Jews and Black Africans have had to fight for recognition of their suffering and acknowledgment of historical injustices. Holocaust denial and attempts to downplay the transatlantic slave trade are examples of efforts to delegitimize the experiences of these communities.

Intersectionality: Many individuals identify as both Jewish and Black, highlighting the intersectionality of these experiences. Such individuals face unique challenges related to discrimination, as they navigate both anti-Semitism and racism.

Role of Diaspora Communities: Diaspora communities of both Jews and Black Africans have played critical roles in advocating for justice and equality. They have served as bridges between their respective communities and host societies and contribute to the broader struggle against discrimination.

Transgenerational Trauma: Both groups have experienced trans-generational trauma resulting from historical injustices. Trauma, passed down through generations, continues to impact the mental health and well-being of individuals in these communities.

Contemporary Solidarity Movements: In recent years, there has been a growing trend of solidarity between Jewish and Black communities. Activists from both backgrounds have come together to address shared concerns related to discrimination, hate crimes, and social justice.

The Importance of Remembering: The shared experiences of Jews and Black Africans emphasize the importance of remembering and learning from history. By acknowledging the injustices of the past, society can strive for a more equitable and compassionate future.

While the experiences of Jews and Black Africans have distinct historical and cultural contexts, these similarities highlight the enduring struggle for justice, equality, and recognition in the face of systemic oppression. Recognizing these shared experiences can foster empathy and solidarity among diverse communities fighting against discrimination and marginalization.

CHAPTER 4
DIFFERENCES IN INJUSTICE AND MARGINALIZATION: JEWS AND BLACK AFRICANS

THE HISTORIES of Jews and Black Africans have been marked by various forms of injustice and marginalization, yet these experiences have been fundamentally different due to distinct historical contexts, geographical locations, and the nature of discrimination they faced. This chapter delves into the key differences in the injustices and marginalization experienced by these two groups.

Historical Context:

Jews: Jewish persecution has deep historical roots, including biblical enslavement in Egypt, the Spanish Inquisition, and pogroms in Europe. These events were often tied to religious differences and suspicions of economic exploitation.

Black Africans: Black Africans experienced centuries of slavery, beginning with the trans-Sahara and transatlantic slave trade and then colonialism. Their marginalization was rooted in racism and the economic exploitation of forced labour on plantations and in mines.

2. Geographical Variation:

Jews: Jewish persecution was often localized to specific regions, such as Europe and the Middle East. While Jews faced discrimination and expulsions in various countries, their experiences varied depending on their location.

Black Africans: The African diaspora resulted in the widespread forceful uprooting and dispersion of Black Africans, leading to the development of distinct experiences in Africa, the Americas, the Caribbean, and elsewhere. The nature of discrimination varied across regions.

Religious vs. Racial Discrimination:

Jews: Discrimination against Jews has historically been rooted in religious differences, with anti-Semitism as a driving force. Accusations of deicide and religious intolerance were central to their persecution.

Black Africans: Marginalization of Black Africans was primarily based on race and physical attributes. The concept of racial superiority and inferiority played a central role in the transatlantic slave trade and colonialism.

Forms of Oppression:

Jews: Jews faced various forms of oppression, including forced conversions, expulsion from countries, and economic restrictions. The Holocaust represented an extreme form of persecution.

Black Africans: Black Africans endured chattel slavery, racial segregation, apartheid, and colonial exploitation. Their oppression often involved systemic violence, dehumanization, and legal discrimination.

Resistance Movements:

Jews: Jewish resistance to persecution included efforts to preserve cultural and religious identity as well as armed resistance in some cases.

Black Africans: Black Africans engaged in numerous resistance movements, from slave rebellions to civil rights struggles and anti-colonial movements, to challenge their oppression.

Legacy and Contemporary Impacts:

Jews: The legacy of Jewish persecution is evident in the Holocaust's enduring trauma, Jewish diaspora communities, and the establishment of Israel.

Black Africans: The legacy of African slavery and colonialism is still felt in racial inequalities, socio-economic disparities, and ongoing struggles for equality and justice.

Nature of Diaspora:

Jews: The Jewish diaspora has been characterized by a strong emphasis on cultural preservation, including the retention of language, religious practices, and traditions. Jewish communities in the diaspora have often maintained close ties to their historical homeland, Israel.

Black Africans: The African diaspora is marked by a dispersion of people across the Americas, the Caribbean, and Europe. While African cultural elements survived, the diaspora led to a broader cultural diversity, with Afro-Caribbean, Afro-Latin, and African American identities emerging.

Colonial Influence:

Jews: Jewish marginalization was not directly linked to colonialism but rather to religious differences and economic factors. While Jews faced expulsion from European countries, they did not experience colonial exploitation.

Black Africans: The marginalization of Black Africans was deeply connected to the colonial era during which European powers subjected African nations to exploitation, forced labour, and cultural erasure. The scars of colonialism continue to impact African nations.

Identity and Self-Determination:

Jews: Jewish identity is rooted in both religious and cultural factors, with a strong emphasis on self-determination through the establishment of Israel as a Jewish homeland.

Black Africans: Black African identity is often shaped by a complex interplay of ethnic, cultural, and national factors; self-determination involves the struggle for political independence from colonial rule.

Modern Forms of Discrimination:

Jews: - In contemporary times, Jews still face anti-Semitism, discrimination, and acts of hatred, though the nature of these forms of discrimination varies across regions.

Black Africans: Discrimination against Black Africans continues globally, manifesting in racial inequalities, systemic racism, and issues such as police violence and social disparities.

In conclusion, while both Jews and Black Africans have experienced significant injustices and marginalization throughout history, their experiences have been distinct due to historical roots, the nature of discrimination, and the impact of colonialism. Recognizing these differences is essential for understanding the unique challenges faced by each group and for addressing the ongoing struggle for equality, justice, and cultural preservation. Both histories serve as powerful reminders of the enduring legacies of historical injustices and the importance of collective efforts to combat discrimination and marginalization.

CHAPTER 5
JEWS HISTORICAL ORIGINS AND EARLY DISPERSAL

THE JEWISH DIASPORA is a historical phenomenon that spans millennia, beginning with the earliest origins of the Jewish people and their dispersion across the ancient world. This chapter explores the roots of the Jewish Diaspora, focusing on the critical periods of exile, particularly the Babylonian and Roman exiles. Understanding these foundational events is essential for appreciating the enduring resilience and cultural richness of the Jewish diaspora communities that have thrived throughout history.

The Origins of the Jewish People:

The origins of the Jewish people are deeply rooted in the biblical narrative. According to Jewish tradition, the Jewish ancestry is traced back to Abraham, who, in the Book of Genesis, was called by God to leave his homeland in Mesopotamia (modern-day Iraq) and settle in the land of Canaan (present-day Israel) 1,400 miles away. Abraham's descendants, including Isaac and Jacob, formed the basis of the twelve tribes of Israel.

1. Tracing the Patriarchs and Matriarchs:

Abraham:

Abraham, often referred to as the "Father of the Jewish People," is a central figure in Jewish tradition. He is believed to have lived around 2000 BCE in the ancient city of Ur in Mesopotamia (modern-day Iraq).

The covenant between Abraham and God is a pivotal event in the Hebrew Bible (Old Testament) and holds immense significance in Judaism, Christianity, and Islam. This covenant is found in the Book of Genesis, primarily in chapters 12, 15, 17, and 22. Here is a summary of the covenant between Abraham and God:

The Call of Abraham (Genesis 12): God calls Abram (later named Abraham) to leave his homeland, Ur of the Chaldeans, and go to the land of Canaan. God promises to make Abram into a great nation, bless him, make his name great, and bless those who bless him.

Abram obeys and journeys to Canaan with his wife Sarai (later named Sarah) and his nephew Lot.

The Promise of Descendants (Genesis 15): God reaffirms the promise to Abram, this time promising him descendants as numerous as the stars. Abram expresses his concern that he has no heir. God assures him that he will have a biological heir and that his descendants will inherit the land of Canaan.

God enters a formal covenant with Abram, symbolized by a vision where animals are divided into two and God passes through them, signifying the binding nature of the covenant.

Sarah and Isaac:

Abraham's wife, Sarah, plays a significant role in the biblical narrative. Despite her initial infertility, she miraculously gives birth to their son, Isaac. Isaac, the second of the Jewish patriarchs, carries forward the covenant established with Abraham.

The Covenant of Circumcision (Genesis 17): God changes Abram's name to Abraham, signifying his role as the father of a multitude of nations. God establishes the covenant of circumcision as a physical sign of the covenant between God and Abraham's descendants.

Sarah's name is also changed and God promises that she will bear a son, Isaac, who will be the heir of the covenant.

The Test of Faith (Genesis 22): God tests Abraham's faith by instructing him to offer his son Isaac as a burnt offering. Abraham, in obedience to God, prepares to carry out the sacrifice but is stopped by an angel of the Lord. God reiterates His promise to bless Abraham's descendants.

The covenant with Abraham is foundational to the Abrahamic religions—Judaism, Christianity, and Islam. It represents God's chosen people (the Jewish people), the promised land (Canaan), and the assurance of blessings for all nations through Abraham's descendants.

In Judaism, Abraham is regarded as the patriarch and a model of faith and obedience. The covenant is commemorated in Jewish rituals and prayers.

In Christianity, Abraham's faith is highlighted in the New Testament, particularly in the Letter to the Romans, where he is described as the father of all who believe. Christians see the covenant's fulfilment in the person of Jesus Christ.

In Islam, Abraham (Ibrahim) is considered a prophet and the covenant is seen as part of the prophetic lineage. The story of Abraham's willingness to sacrifice his son is also significant in Islamic tradition.

In summary, the covenant between God and Abraham is a foundational narrative in the monotheistic faiths, emphasising faith, obedience, and the promise of blessings to all nations through Abraham's descendants.

Jacob (Israel) and the Twelve Tribes: Isaac's son, Jacob, later known as Israel, becomes the father of twelve sons. These twelve sons and their descendants form the twelve tribes of Israel, each of which plays a unique role in the history and traditions of the Jewish people.

2 Exodus and Wilderness Wanderings: The biblical account of the Jewish people entering and exiting Egypt is a central narrative in Jewish history and is primarily found in the book of Exodus in the Hebrew Bible, known as the Old Testament in Christian tradition. This narrative encompasses several key events and figures, including Moses, Pharaoh, and the Exodus itself. Here is a summarized account:

Entering Egypt: The biblical story of the Jews entering the land of Egypt is a pivotal episode in the larger narrative of Jewish history. Found in the Book of Genesis, it sets the stage for a series of events that would ultimately shape the destiny of the Jewish people. This narrative revolves around Joseph, one of the twelve sons of Jacob (also known as Israel), and his journey from Canaan to Egypt. It not only illustrates the theme of divine providence but also foreshadows the Jews' sojourn in Egypt, leading to their eventual enslavement and, ultimately, their Exodus.

The story begins with Joseph, the favoured son of Jacob, who is sold into slavery by his jealous brothers. Joseph is taken to Egypt, where he is sold to Potiphar, an Egyptian official. Joseph's extraordinary ability to interpret dreams eventually brings him to the attention of Pharaoh, the ruler of Egypt. Through divine guidance, Joseph predicts a seven-year period of plenty followed by a seven-year famine.

Joseph's interpretation of Pharaoh's dream leads to his appointment as a high-ranking official in Egypt who is responsible for preparing for the coming famine. During this time, Joseph's family in Canaan also suffers from the famine. Jacob, now an old man, sends his remaining sons to Egypt to buy grain. Unbeknownst to them, they come before Joseph, who recognizes them but remains incognito. Over time, Joseph reveals his identity to his brothers and reunites with his father, Jacob.

Pharaoh, upon learning of Joseph's family, extends an invitation for Jacob and his sons to settle in Egypt, specifically in the land of Goshen, where they can graze their flocks. Jacob, grateful for Pharaoh's generosity and seeing the opportunity to escape the famine, accepts the offer. Thus, the Israelites enter Egypt and begin their sojourn in the land.

The narrative of Joseph's journey to Egypt underscores the theme of divine providence throughout the Bible. It depicts how God's plan unfolds through the lives of individuals, even in the face of adversity and hardship. Furthermore, this narrative foreshadows the later events in the Book of Exodus, where the Israelites' status in Egypt changes from being guests to becoming enslaved under a new Pharaoh who "did not know Joseph."

Over time, a new Pharaoh arises who does not know Joseph and becomes fearful of the Hebrew population's growth. In response, Pharaoh enslaves the Hebrews, subjecting them to harsh labour and oppression.

Birth and Early Life of Moses: In this context, a Hebrew baby named Moses is born. His mother places him in a basket and sets him adrift in the Nile River to save his life. He is discovered and adopted by Pharaoh's daughter, who names him Moses.

The Call of Moses: As an adult, Moses becomes aware of his Hebrew heritage and is called by God through a burning bush to lead the Israelites out of Egypt and to the Promised Land, a land flowing with milk and honey.

Plagues and Hardening of Pharaoh's Heart: Moses, along with his brother Aaron, confronts Pharaoh and demands the release of the Israelites. When Pharaoh refuses, a series of ten devastating plagues are unleashed on Egypt, including the Nile turning to blood, frogs, gnats, flies, livestock disease, boils, hail, locusts, darkness, and the death of the firstborn.

Despite the plagues, Pharaoh repeatedly hardens his heart and refuses to let the Israelites go, leading to further suffering and loss in Egypt.

The Passover and Exodus: Before the final plague, God instructs the Israelites to sacrifice a lamb and mark their doorposts with its blood. This act of faith and obedience is known as the Passover. That night, the Angel of Death passes over the homes of the Israelites, sparing their firstborn, but taking the firstborn of Egypt.

Pharaoh, devastated by the death of his own son, finally relents and allows the Israelites to leave Egypt. The Israelites hastily prepare for their departure, taking unleavened bread and their possessions.

Crossing the Red Sea: As the Israelites depart, Pharaoh changes his mind once more and pursues them with his army. The Israelites find themselves trapped between the Egyptian army and the Red Sea. God miraculously parts the waters of the Red Sea, allowing the Israelites to cross on dry land. When the Egyptian army attempts to pursue, the waters return, drowning them.

This narrative of the Exodus from Egypt holds immense significance in Jewish tradition. It symbolises liberation from oppression, the covenant between God and the Jewish people, and the journey toward the Promised Land. The Passover holiday, celebrated annually, commemorates these events, and reinforces their enduring importance in Jewish identity and faith.

3. The Conquest of Canaan:

The Covenant at Mount Sinai:

A pivotal moment in the Exodus narrative occurs at Mount Sinai where Moses receives the Ten Commandments and the Mosaic Covenant from God. The covenant established a set of laws and principles that continue to shape Jewish religious and ethical life.

Forty Years in the Wilderness:

Following the Exodus and the crossing of the Red Sea, the Israelites embark on a forty-year journey through the wilderness. During this time, they receive further divine guidance, including the construction of the Tabernacle, a portable sanctuary.

The Longing for the Promised Land: Throughout their wilderness wanderings, the Israelites long for the Promised Land of Canaan, where God promised to lead them.

The journey represents a test of faith and a period of spiritual growth for the Israelites.

4. Settlement in Canaan:

Crossing the Jordan River: Under the leadership of Joshua, Moses' successor, the Israelites cross the Jordan River to enter the land of Canaan. The miraculous parting of the Jordan River echoed the earlier miracle at the Red Sea.

The Conquest of Canaan: The conquest of Canaan involves military campaigns, the capture of key cities like Jericho, and alliances with local tribes. The Israelites seek to establish their presence and fulfil God's promise of the land.

Twelve Tribes and Tribal Allotments: Canaan is divided among the twelve tribes of Israel, each receiving a portion of the land. This division creates a decentralized system of governance and contributed to the tribal identities within Israel.

1. The Kingdoms of Israel and Judah:

The establishment of the Kingdoms of Israel and Judah occurred during a period of significant geopolitical and cultural change in the ancient Near East. These kingdoms played a pivotal role in shaping the identity, religious practices, and historical memory of the Jewish people.

The United Kingdom: The United Kingdom of Israel emerged under the leadership of King Saul, followed by King David and his son King Solomon. This era, known as the Davidic-Solomonic monarchy, is often regarded as a time of political consolidation and territorial expansion

The Kingdom of Israel (Northern Kingdom): After the death of Solomon, the United Kingdom split into the northern Kingdom of Israel and the southern Kingdom of Judah. The northern kingdom, centred in Samaria, retained the name Israel and its capital at various times.

The Kingdom of Judah (Southern Kingdom): The southern Kingdom of Judah, with its capital in Jerusalem, included the territories of the tribes of Judah and Benjamin. Jerusalem held particular religious significance as the site of the First Temple, a central place of worship and pilgrimage.

Religious Developments: During this period, religious practices evolved and the role of the prophets became prominent in guiding the moral and ethical conduct of the people. The construction of the First Temple under Solomon represented a culmination of religious aspirations.

Division and Exile: The division between Israel and Judah persisted for several centuries, marked by shifting alliances, conflicts, and the influence of neighbouring empires. Ultimately, the Assyrian conquest of the northern Kingdom of Israel in 722 BCE and the Babylonian exile of the southern Kingdom of Judah in 586 BCE were watershed moments in Jewish history.

Impact on Jewish Identity: Despite the eventual fall of both kingdoms and the exile of many Israelites and Judeans, the memory of the united and divided kingdoms remained deeply ingrained in Jewish collective memory. The biblical narratives, historical records, and religious teachings associated with this period continue to shape Jewish identity and provide lessons in faith, morality, and resilience.

In conclusion, the origins of the Jewish people are deeply intertwined with the biblical narrative, especially with Abraham as a central figure whose covenant with God laid the groundwork for Jewish faith and identity. The subsequent generations of patriarchs and matriarchs, the exodus from Egypt, and the conquest of Canaan are key elements of the Jewish story. These early foundations, characterized by faith, covenant, and ethical principles, continue to be central to Jewish identity and practice and serve as a source of inspiration and guidance for Jewish communities worldwide.

THE IMPACT OF THE DISPERSAL ON THE DESCENDANTS OF ISAAC AND ISHMAEL

The biblical figures Isaac and Ishmael, as the sons of Abraham, hold a significant place in the Abrahamic faiths of Judaism, Christianity, and Islam. Understanding their contemporary populations and the reasons for variations is not only an exercise in demography but also a reflection of the historical, religious, dispersion and geopolitical factors that have shaped their communities over millennia. This section explores the current populations of the descendants of Isaac and Ishmael and delves into the reasons behind the variations.

I. Isaac: The Lineage of Promise

1. **Historical Context:** According to the Bible, Isaac was born to Abraham and Sarah when they were well advanced in age after God's promise to make Abraham a father of many nations. Isaac is considered the father of the Israelites, the chosen people in Judaism.
2. **Contemporary Jewish Population:** As of 2021, the global Jewish population is estimated to be approximately 14 million. This population is distributed worldwide, with significant communities in Israel, the United States, and various European countries.
3. **Factors Influencing Population Growth:** The growth of the Jewish population can be attributed to natural population increase, dispersal, immigration to Israel (known as Aliyah), and a relatively high birth rate among Orthodox Jewish communities.

II. Ishmael: The Lineage of Many Nations

1. **Historical Context:** Ishmael was born to Abraham and Hagar, Sarah's Egyptian maidservant. According to Islamic tradition, Ishmael is considered a prophet and the father of the Arab people.
2. **Contemporary Arab Population:** The Arab world comprises 22 countries across the Middle East and North Africa (MENA) region. As of 2021, the Arab population is estimated to be over 400 million, making it one of the most populous ethnic groups globally.
3. **Factors Influencing Population Growth:** The growth of the Arab population is driven by a combination of factors, including high fertility rates, improved healthcare, and a relatively young population. Additionally, urbanization and economic opportunities have led to population concentration in urban areas.

III. The impact of dispersal on Jewish population

The impact of dispersal on reducing the overall Jewish population is a complex and multifaceted historical phenomenon. While the Jewish Diaspora has indeed led to the dispersion of Jewish communities across the globe, it is important to note that the primary drivers of population changes among Jews have been influenced by various factors, including natural population growth, assimilation, migration, and historical events. Here are some key factors to consider:

Natural population Decline: Dispersal can directly influence population growth or decline. When individuals or groups move to a new area, they can contribute to the growth of the population in that region. Conversely, if people leave a particular area, it can lead to a decline in the local population. Like any other population, Jewish communities have experienced natural population growth over time. Birth rates, mortality rates, and family size have all played a role in determining population trends.

Assimilation: Assimilation refers to the process by which individuals from minority groups adopt the customs, culture, and sometimes the religion of the dominant society. Assimilation has led to individuals and families leaving the Jewish community, which can impact the overall Jewish population in some regions.

Demographic Changes: Dispersal often leads to changes in the demographic composition of populations. For example, migration can affect age distribution, family structures, and cultural practices. Jewish migration, both voluntary and forced, has had a significant impact on the size and distribution of Jewish populations. Events such as the Babylonian exile, the Jewish expulsion from Spain in 1492, and Jewish immigration to the United States and Israel have all shaped population dynamics.

Economic and Social Impact: Dispersal can impact the economic and social dynamics of both the areas of departure and arrival. In areas with significant emigration, there may be a loss of labour force and talent, potentially leading to economic challenges and reduction in birth rate.

Persecution and Genocide: Tragic events such as the Holocaust during World War II resulted in the loss of millions of Jewish lives. This catastrophic event had a devastating impact on Jewish populations in Europe and beyond.

Return to Israel: The establishment of the State of Israel in 1948 marked a significant demographic shift. Jewish communities worldwide have seen varying rates of emigration to Israel, a phenomenon known as Aliyah. This has both reduced the Jewish populations in their countries of origin and increased the Jewish population in Israel.

Conflict and Tensions: Large-scale dispersal, such as mass migration, can have environmental consequences. Increased population density in certain areas can lead to resource depletion, deforestation, and habitat destruction, impacting local ecosystems. Dispersal can sometimes lead to social tensions and conflicts, especially when there is competition for limited resources or differences in cultural norms and values. Displaced populations may face discrimination or xenophobia in their new locations.

Intermarriage: Intermarriage between Jews and individuals from other religious or ethnic backgrounds has been a subject of demographic concern.

In summary, while the Jewish Diaspora has resulted in the dispersion of Jewish communities, the impact on reducing the overall Jewish population has been influenced by a complex interplay of factors. Natural population growth, assimilation, migration, historical events, and religious dynamics have all played roles in shaping the size and distribution of Jewish populations. It is essential to consider these factors when analysing changes in the Jewish population over time.

CHAPTER 6
THE HISTORICAL RELATIONSHIP BETWEEN JEWISH PEOPLE AND BLACK PEOPLE

THE HISTORICAL RELATIONSHIP between Jewish people and Black people, as depicted in the Bible, is a topic that has been the subject of various interpretations and debates as the Bible itself does not categorize individuals by race as we understand it today. Instead, the Bible focuses on historical, religious, and cultural narratives.

However, some passages and figures in the Bible are often associated with individuals or regions that some scholars believe may have had African or black origins. Here are some references and figures frequently discussed in this context:

The Queen of Sheba: The Queen of Sheba is mentioned in the Old Testament, particularly in 1 Kings 10 and 2 Chronicles 9. She is traditionally associated with the region of Sheba, which is believed to be in modern-day Ethiopia or Yemen. Her visit to King Solomon has led to discussions about her potential African or black heritage.

Cush and Cushites: The term "Cush" appear in the Bible, often referring to a region that is believed to have included parts of modern-day Sudan and Ethiopia. Cushites are mentioned in various biblical passages, such as Numbers 12:1 and Jeremiah 13:23. Some scholars associate Cushites with black African origins.

The Ethiopian Eunuch: In the New Testament, Acts 8:26-40 tells the story of an Ethiopian eunuch who encounters Philip and becomes a Christian. This narrative is sometimes cited in discussions of black individuals in the Bible.

The "Song of Solomon" Beloved: The Song of Solomon, also known as the Song of Songs, contains poetic descriptions of the beloved's physical appearance, including references to her skin being "black" and "beautiful" (Song of Solomon 1:5-6). Interpretations of this passage vary and is understood in the context of poetic and symbolic language.

Joseph's Marriage to an Egyptian: In Genesis 41:45, it is mentioned that Joseph, one of Jacob's sons, married an Egyptian woman named Asenath. This highlights a connection between the Israelites and Egypt.

The Mixed Multitude during the Exodus: During the Exodus, a "mixed multitude" is mentioned in Exodus 12:38 as accompanying the Israelites as they left Egypt. This suggests a diverse group of people, including Egyptians, who joined the Israelites in their journey.

Zipporah: Zipporah, the wife of Moses, is described as a "Cushite" woman in Numbers 12:1. This description has led to discussions about her potential African or black heritage. For example, Numbers 12:1 describes how Miriam and Aaron spoke against Moses for marrying a Cushite woman.

Ezekiel's Description of Egypt: In the Book of Ezekiel, there are vivid descriptions of Egypt, including references to the Egyptians as having "beautiful legs" and "colourful robes" (Ezekiel 23:6-8). These descriptions provide insights into Ezekiel's perceptions of the Egyptians.

References to Tarshish: Tarshish is mentioned in the Old Testament as a distant maritime location known for its wealth and trade (e.g., Jonah 1:3). While the exact location of Tarshish is debated among scholars, some propose that it could have had connections to regions outside the Mediterranean, including parts of Africa.

Ebed-Melech's Role in Jeremiah's Rescue: Ebed-Melech, the Ethiopian, is noted for his compassion and bravery in rescuing the prophet Jeremiah from a cistern (Jeremiah 38:7-13). His story illustrates positive interactions between different ethnic groups.

Simon of Cyrene: In the Synoptic Gospels (Matthew 27:32, Mark 15:21, and Luke 23:26), Simon of Cyrene is mentioned as the man who carried the cross of Jesus on the way to the crucifixion. Cyrene was a Greek city in North Africa, and some interpretations suggest that Simon may have had African or black origins.

Simeon called Niger: In Acts 13:1, a figure named Simeon is mentioned, referred to as "Simeon who was called Niger." The term "Niger" means "black" in Latin, leading some to speculate about his potential African heritage.

Apollos: In Acts 18:24-28, Apollos is described as an eloquent and learned man from Alexandria. Alexandria was a prominent city in Egypt, and Apollos may have had Egyptian or African connections.

Candace, Queen of the Ethiopians: In Acts 8:27, the Ethiopian eunuch mentioned earlier is described as a eunuch "in charge of all the treasure of the queen of the Ethiopians." This reference suggests the presence of significant African political and cultural influence.

The Diverse Crowd at Pentecost: In Acts 2:9-11, the crowd that gathered at Pentecost is described as including people from various regions, including "Egypt and the parts of Libya belonging to Cyrene." This indicates the presence of people from North Africa in the early Christian community.

It's important to reiterate that while these references provide glimpses into the diversity of the early Christian community and interactions with individuals from various regions, the New Testament primarily focuses on religious and theological narratives. Discussions of race or ethnicity as modern classifications were not the primary concerns of the biblical authors.

CHAPTER 7
TRACING AFRICAN DIASPORA EARLY MIGRATIONS AND CIVILIZATIONS

THE AFRICAN DIASPORA is a complex and multifaceted historical phenomenon that spans thousands of years and is characterized by the migration, dispersion, and settlement of African peoples across the world. To understand the roots of this vast diaspora, it is essential to trace the earliest migrations of African peoples and the emergence of various African civilizations. This chapter delves into these historical foundations and sheds light on the rich and diverse tapestry of African history.

I. Early Migrations of African Peoples:

African Homo sapiens: Genetic and archaeological scholars believe that the human species evolved on the continent of Africa. Therefore, Africa is considered the cradle of humanity, where early Homo sapiens evolved and began to migrate to other continents.

Archaeologists believe the fire was first lit in East Africa around two million years ago and this discovery remains one of the most ground-breaking events in the development of humanity. Fire gave humans an advantage over all other animals: they could cook with it, which aided in the quick digestion and absorption of most of their food, making digestion faster. Unlike other predators, which had to sleep for hours to digest their raw food, man could stay awake longer. Staying awake longer meant humans could think longer, be more creative, and keep warm in all environments. Staying awake gave humans the time to discover fishing and develop language, art, paint-making as well as develop collective learning of hunting animals, gathering edible plants, and making ornaments.

Palaeolithic and Neolithic migrations refer to the movement of human populations during two distinct periods of prehistoric history: the Palaeolithic Era and the Neolithic Era.

Palaeolithic Migrations (2.6 million years ago to 10,000 BCE): There are suggestions that after the human ancestors began to walk and shed most of their body hairs, they quickly evolved dark skin for protection against U.V. radiation from the Sun. As a result, all humans were originally black; white skin only appeared in higher frequencies around 8,000 years ago. DNA evidence shows that skeletons from earlier than 8,000 years in Spain, Hungary, and Luxembourg (Central and Southern Europe) were brown-skinned. An example is the Cheddar man, the oldest skeleton of the human species found in the United Kingdom, in Somerset, in the heart of Britain. His genetic markers indicated that he was dark-skinned, with dark brown hair and blue eyes. The Cheddar man is an early indication that Africans or descendants did live in Europe and were a part of its population. Cheddar man is believed to have lived 10,000 years ago.

Paleolithic Hunter-Gatherers: Throughout the Paleolithic Era, Homo sapiens (modern humans) lived as nomadic hunter-gatherers. They followed migratory patterns of animals and seasonal food sources, moving in small groups to ensure their survival.

Land Bridges and Coastal Routes: During periods of lower sea levels, land bridges, such as the Bering Land Bridge (Beringia), connected continents. This allowed human populations to migrate between Asia and the Americas as well as between Asia and Australia.

The "Out of Africa" Theory: Genetic and archaeological evidence supports the idea that modern humans migrated from Africa to populate other parts of the world, starting around 70,000 years ago.

Neolithic Migrations (10,000 BCE to 2,000 BCE):

Agricultural Revolution: The Neolithic Era marked the transition from hunting and gathering to agriculture and settled farming communities. This revolution occurred independently in different regions around the world, including the Fertile Crescent, China, Mesoamerica, and West Africa.

Sedentary Lifestyle: With the development of agriculture, people began to settle in one place, cultivating crops and domesticating animals. This led to population growth and the establishment of permanent villages and towns.

Spread of Agricultural Practices: As farming techniques and technologies improved, knowledge of agriculture spread through migration and cultural diffusion. Agricultural practices, along with the domestication of plants and animals, travelled from one region to another.

Impact of Migration on Human History:

The Neolithic Revolution and subsequent migrations laid the foundation for more complex societies, the development of civilization, and the growth of human populations.

Overall, Paleolithic and Neolithic migrations played a crucial role in shaping human history, from the dispersal of early Homo species within (Bantu Migration) and out of Africa to the emergence of settled agricultural communities and the eventual rise of civilizations. These migrations were driven by the fundamental human need for sustenance and the adaptation to changing environments over millennia.

1. Bantu Migration in Africa

Bantu Migration: The Bantu-speaking peoples, originating in West Africa in the region that is now modern-day Nigeria and Cameroon, embarked on a significant migration around 2000 BCE. Over several centuries, the Bantu migration reached the southern tip of Africa and brought with it agricultural and ironworking technologies that profoundly influenced the continent's history.

The Bantu migration is one of the most significant population movements in African history as it involves the expansion of Bantu-speaking peoples across a large part of the African continent. They migrated both southward, along the eastern and western coasts of Africa, and eastward into central and southern Africa. This migration occurred over thousands of years, from around 1000 BCE to 1500 CE, and had a profound impact on the cultural, linguistic, and demographic landscape of Africa.

The Bantu migration was driven by several factors, including population growth, the search for new agricultural lands, the spread of ironworking technology, and possibly climate changes. Ironworking was a crucial technological advancement that allowed Bantu communities to clear forests and cultivate new lands and thus increase agricultural productivity. Bantu agricultural practices, including the cultivation of crops like millet, sorghum, yams, and bananas, had a transformative effect on the economies and societies of the areas they settled.

Impact of the Bantu migration in Africa:

As Bantu-speaking groups migrated and settled in new regions, they formed a wide variety of societies, from small-scale communities to complex chiefdoms and kingdoms. The development of organized societies was often linked to agriculture and trade.

The Bantu migration reshaped the demographic and linguistic map of Africa and contributed to the diversity of African cultures and societies. The Bantu migration played a role in the formation of states and empires in Africa's history.

The Bantu migration is a testament to the adaptability, resourcefulness, and agricultural innovations of Bantu-speaking peoples. It had a lasting impact on the cultural, linguistic, and historical tapestry of Africa and its legacy can still be seen today in the diversity of African societies and languages.

THE EMERGENCE OF VARIOUS AFRICAN CIVILIZATIONS

Ancient Egypt:

Egypt was the oldest African culture, which rose to eminence and had the first recorded monarch in human history. Egyptologists agreed that ancient Egypt started around 4,500 BC. The ancient Africans built the city of Memphis in ancient Egypt in 3100 B.C., which was nearly 2000 years before any European civilisation, for example, the Greeks built Athens in 1200 B.C., and the Romans built Rome in 1000 B.C.

The early Egyptian civilization had to invent things for themselves from scratch because they were the pioneer of many discoveries. They were the first to discover metallurgy, astronomy, writing, paper, medicine, mechanics & machinery (including ramps, levers, ploughs and mills) and all that is needed for the continuation of a large, organized society. Their exploration of the different fields of studies allowed them to create iconic inventions such as the pyramids.

Hierogslyphs from Egypt

THE KINGDOM OF NUBIA

This is a region along the Nile River in present-day Sudan. Nubia was another African region regarded as the Land of Great Natural Wealth and the world's envy. Scholars were fascinated by the ruins of large red-brick churches and monasteries, which had murals and frescoes of fine quality. Skilled labour was involved in making the bricks, the paintings, and the architecture. The military organization centred on archery as the infantry was mostly equipped with swords, axes, clubs, and shields. Weapons during this period were made of bronze. Nubia and Egypt date far back into history in terms of relating against each other than in alliances.

THE KINGDOM OF AXUM AROUND ETHIOPIA.

Axum was founded near the Red Sea coast from 100 AD to 940 AD. The city of Aksum is the seventh oldest continuously inhabited city in Africa, with the first signs of human inhabitancy dating back to 400 BC. The Empire of Axum, at times, extended across most of present-day Eritrea, northern Ethiopia, Western Yemen, and parts of eastern Sudan. The capital city of the empire was Axum, now in northern Ethiopia. The Emperor of Ethiopia was addressed as 'Conquering Lion of the Tribe of Judah, Elect of God, King of Kings'. As mentioned earlier, the biblical accounts of this royal meeting are found in the Bible, 1st Kings and 2nd Chronicles 2.

GHANA EMPIRE

Ghana Empire (4th-13th centuries CE): Flourishing due to its control of the trans-Saharan trade routes, the empire was renowned for its wealth, culture, and sophisticated governance structures, including a centralised bureaucracy and a system of regional governors. The kingdom covered 250,000 square kilometres and ruled a population of 3 million. Ghana Empire was the first major agricultural empire to arise in the Sahel region. Traders referred to Ghana as "the Land of Gold". Archaeologist believes that, around 300 CE, West Africans domesticated the camel as an efficient form of transport across the desert. Camels revolutionised the trade across the Sahara.

MALI EMPIRE

The Mali Empire was an empire in West Africa from c. 1235 to 1670. The Mali Empire was once one of Africa's largest, richest, and most powerful empires. The Mali empire in the 1300s was the size of western Europe alone. It went from the Atlantic coast to the Niger River and included many of the western Sahara desert trade towns. Unknown to many, Mali was a centre of civilisation and Timbuktu University was the first university in the world. The city of Timbuktu (present-day Mali) in the 14th century was five times bigger than the city of London. It was the wealthiest city in the world and had the richest man in the history of humanity. At the time of his death in 1331, Mansa Musa was worth the equivalent of 400 billion dollars (twice the worth of Jeff Bezos' net worth of $213.11 billion in 2021).

SONGHAI EMPIRE

Songhai Empire (15th-16th centuries CE): The Songhai Empire succeeded Mali and became one of the largest empires in African history, known for its centralized administration and scholarly achievements.

BENIN EMPIRE AND THE GREAT WALLS OF BENIN

The Great precolonial Benin kingdom is one of the oldest West African civilisations in existence from 355 BC to the present. The kingdom is recognised for its brilliant bronze, ivory, and iron artefacts and military prowess. The old Benin city is still in the present-day location of Benin city in Edo state, South-west Nigeria. When the Europeans first arrived at the Benin kingdom in the late 15th Century, they were astonished by the wealth, quality of life, and its organization. The Dutch writer Olfert Dapper wrote the following in Dutch and translated it into English, an account of merchants who had seen Benin:

> *"Benin City is at least four miles wide. The city has wide, straight roads lined by houses. The houses are large and handsome, with walls made from clay. The people are very friendly and there seems to be no stealing. Inside the city is the king's court. It is large and square and surrounded by a wall. The court is divided into many palaces with separate houses and apartments for courtiers.*
>
> *The court has many galleries flanked by wooden pillars. Fixed to these pillars are shining metal plaques showing battle scenes and deeds of courage."*

Massive walls and deep ditches surrounded Benin city, which stretched beyond the city walls. The structure, upon completion, comprised of ditches and ramparts, covered a border distance of about 16,000 kilometres and enclosed about 6,500 square kilometres of community land. Altogether this was double the length of the Ming Great Wall of China, which measured 8,851 kilometres.

OYO EMPIRE

Oyo Empire is a West African monarchy that, at its peak, covered 270,000 square kilometres. The Oyo Empire was a powerful Yoruba state in what is now western Nigeria. It began in the 1300s in the West African savannah north of the tropical forests where other Yoruba peoples lived. Being in the savannah proved beneficial as Oyo could use horses obtained from North Africa for the cavalry. Using armoured cavalry, the empire was able to extend its reach across parts of what is now northern and western Nigeria.

KINGDOM OF ZIMBABWE (1220-1450 AD)

The word Zimbabwe can be loosely translated to 'House of Rock'. The Kingdom of Zimbabwe controlled the ivory and gold trade from the interior to the southeastern coast of Africa. One of the significant constructions in Zimbabwe is brick (dated around the 14th century). The Zimbabwean people built mainly with stone and mud. They had perfected the technique of cutting and shaping the stone in such a way that the stones could be stacked in a wall perfectly without the use of mortar, and the wall would hold its shape and integrity. Skill, creativity, and artistry went into the construction of the walls, especially concerning the decorations, the inner recesses and the doors.

Dzimba dza mabwe – house of stone

In conclusion, the African Diaspora is rooted in ancient migrations and diverse civilizations that flourished across the African continent. These early movements and cultures laid the foundation for the rich tapestry of African history, contributing to the development of global trade networks, the spread of religions, and the exchange of ideas and cultures. Understanding these origins is crucial for comprehending the enduring legacy of the African Diaspora and the significant impact of African peoples on the world throughout history.

CHAPTER 8
THE AFRICAN DISPLACEMENT: IMPACTS AND ROUTES:

SLAVERY IS one of human history's most terrible crimes and injustices - the treatment of human beings as property and the deprivation of personal rights. Slavery occurred in almost every ancient civilization, including ancient Egypt, ancient China, Persia, ancient Greece, the Roman Empire, the Arab Islamic Caliphate, and Sultanate. Typically, ancient slavery consists of a mixture of debt-slavery, punishment for crime, prisoners of war, child abandonment, and children born to slaves. This form of slavery, however, pales in comparison to what transpired in Africa from the 7th century to the 20th century.

Two major slave trades took place in Africa:

1. The trans-Saharan slave trade
2. The trans-Atlantic slave trade

THE TRANS-SAHARAN SLAVE TRADE

The trans-Saharan slave trade started when the Arabs began to invade Africa in large numbers from 749 CE and settled in Alexandria, Egypt. The Arabs were mistakenly perceived by Africans as cousins and were welcomed as saviours from the oppressive rule of Byzantium (Graeco-Roman or Christian domination). The Arabs did not initially force their religion on the African Egyptians, but the Qur'an could not be translated into local languages like the Bible. As a result, literacy in Arabic soon spread and was assisted by intermarriages, and Islam soon became the land's religion.

After the Arabs had conquered Egypt and shortly after Muhammad's death, they began demanding Nubian slaves from the south, which continued for 600 years. Dominated African kingdoms were forced to regularly send tributes of enslaved people to the Arab ruler in Cairo. From as early as the 6th century CE, Arabs had developed slavery supply networks out of Africa, from the Sahara to the Red Sea as well as from Ethiopia, Somalia, and East Africa to feed demands for slaves all over the Arab world and the Indian Ocean region.

Between 650 CE and 1905 CE, over 10,000,000 African slaves were delivered through the Trans Sahara route alone to the Arab world and millions died on route. Enslaved African women were sold to households as sex labour and offspring from the illicit encounters were primarily destroyed. Most of the Zanjs (Black) male slaves were transported to Lower Iraq. The enslaved African men were castrated and used as servants to do the meanest and hardest work at the Sahara salt deposits all over the Arab world.

This trade-in African slaves, begun by the Arabs, went on uninterrupted from the 6th century CE to the 15th century CE. It softened Africa militarily, culturally, economically, socially and politically, for the joint European and Arab onslaught on African people and economy from the 15th century CE onwards. The chaos and devastation that followed the invasions finally set up Africa for the intense European slave trade.

THE TRANSATLANTIC SLAVE TRADE

The African experience during the transatlantic slave trade is a harrowing chapter in world history, marked by the brutal subjugation, forced migration, and exploitation of millions of Africans. This section chronicles the African experience during this period, including the transatlantic slave trade, the nightmarish Middle Passage, and the horrors of chattel slavery in the Americas. Understanding this dark period is essential to appreciating the resilience and contributions of African diaspora communities today.

The transatlantic slave trade, lasting from the 15th to the 19th centuries, involved the mass trafficking of Africans to the Americas, primarily for forced labour on plantations. European powers, particularly Portugal, Spain, Britain, France, and the Netherlands, established vast trading networks and profited from the sale of African captives.

The Trans-Atlantic Slave trade is the most infamous case of human trafficking in human history. It stands out because of its global scale. At least 12.5 million Africans were taken from their homes and shipped across the Atlantic to the Americas between 1532 and

1832. They were forced to work until they died for landowners who 'owned' them.

The transatlantic slave trade started when the Portuguese used their economic and strategic naval advantages to navigate around west Africa to the Cape of Good Hope, South Africa, in 1495. After reaching the Indian Ocean, the Portuguese started kidnapping people from the west coast of Africa and took them as a slave to Portugal so that by the middle of the 16th century, more than 10% of Lisbon's population were of African descent.

The Atlantic Slave Trade expanded to America for economic reasons. Many factors exacerbated the demand for African slaves following the European discovery of the size of the wealth of America:

1. The Europeans that travelled to America were too few and were not physically strong enough to handle the pressure of farming in tropical weather with basic farming tools.
2. The European exploration of America brought with it the introduction of foreign and deadly diseases to the native populations of America (the Red Indians). As many as 80% of Native Americans died from diseases brought by the Europeans.
3. The Indians of America who remained after the epidemy were not used to farming intensively. Most of the captured native Indians ran away or disappeared from the plantations as they knew the terrain well.
4. The Europeans decided to turn to Africa for cheap labour to set up a colony since Africa was the nearest continent that had a strong and healthy population and a well-established agriculture system that only required basic tools. The Africans were also a disciplined labour force and were able to work in the mosquito-infested plantation.

Europeans started to promote slavery among kingdoms in Africa by offering guns, alcohol, and manufactured goods to already established Arab slavers and African tribal leaders in return for abducting people to be traded as slaves. Selling slaves to European companies also allowed the tribal leaders to build up their kingdoms and set them apart from their rivals.

The slave trade was later backed by international trade between Africa and Europe. African kingdoms and rulers were also complicit in the slave trade as they traded captives from rival tribes for European goods. However, many Africans were captured through violence, deception, and raids by European and African enslavers.

A 2014 estimate based on the slave voyages database suggests the number of slaves transported across the Atlantic was over 12.5 million; about 77 percent of these slaves (10.1 million) were from the countries of Togo, Benin, Nigeria, the Democratic Republic of Congo, Angola, and the Gold Coast (Ghana). However, this figure only represents the number of African slaves that landed alive in the Americas, the Atlantic islands, and Europe.

The author of "The Slave Trade", Patrick Manning estimates that about 1.5 million died on board ships (others have estimated ship deaths at 2.2 million) and 4 million died inside Africa during the raid, the capture, and in transit from the interior to the coast.

Slaves often travelled in Africa for many miles on foot in coffles - lines of captives shackled or bound together . The reality of the slave caravans was written by the British explorer Mungo Park in the 1790s.

> '..... a typical column of slaves would spend eight hours a day on the road, covering about 20 miles. They were joined in pairs at the leg, and a chain would attach them, one to another, at the neck".... 'they are doomed to a life of captivity in a foreign land'.

Most of the captives resisted being transported to the ships lying at anchor on the open seas. One slave-ship captain, Thomas Phillips, left this account:

> *"When our slaves came to the seaside, our canoes were ready to carry them off to the longboat if the sea permitted, and she conveyed them aboard ship, where the men were all put in irons, two and two shackled together, to prevent their mutiny or swimming ashore. The negroes are so wilful and loathe to leave their own country that they have often leapt out of canoes, boats and ships into the sea and kept underwater till they drowned to avoid being taken up and saved ... they are having a more dreadful apprehension of Barbados than we of hell ...*

The average slaving voyage to the Americas took six to eight weeks. The ships' crews used iron muzzles and whips to exert control. The separation of male and female and the levels of violence and aggression aboard slave ships made acts of physical and sexual abuse by the sailors a feature of all voyages.

The loss of life was high on all voyages, particularly during the first part, when disease and psychological trauma were especially lethal. When the disease began to spread, there was a tendency to throw the sicker Africans overboard.

The Middle Passage refers to the nightmarish journey that millions of Africans endured during the transatlantic slave trade. It was a brutal and harrowing voyage from Africa to the Americas, marked by unimaginable suffering, death, and dehumanization.

Here are some of the appalling conditions on slave ships:

1. Overcrowding: Enslaved Africans were crammed into the holds of slave ships with little regard for their comfort or safety. The available space was extremely limited and there was often not enough room for individuals to sit or lie down comfortably. The slaves were chained together with less than 1 metre (100 cm) in which to sit up in. Male slaves were usually shackled together at the foot. In theory, each man was allotted a space of 1.8m (6ft) by 0.4m (1ft 4in). This overcrowding exacerbated the spread of diseases and made movement nearly impossible

Slaves being loaded into ships on the west coast of Africa Source: BBC.com

2. Chained and Shackled: Enslaved Africans were routinely chained and shackled to prevent resistance or escape. These restraints were uncomfortable and often caused physical injuries as individuals were unable to move freely for the duration of the journey.

3. Filthy and Unsanitary Conditions: The holds of slave ships were filthy and unsanitary. Human waste, vomit, and other bodily fluids mixed with limited food and water, creating an environment ripe for the spread of diseases. The lack of proper sanitation led to the rapid transmission of illnesses.

4. Lack of Ventilation: The holds were often poorly ventilated, with little fresh air or sunlight. This lack of ventilation contributed to the stifling heat, foul odors, and the spread of diseases. The darkness and confinement added to the psychological trauma experienced by the enslaved.

5. Inadequate Food and Water: Enslaved Africans received meager rations of food and water. The food provided was often of poor quality and insufficient to sustain their health. Food consisted mostly of starch: biscuit, flour, yam and beans flavoured with palm oil and hot peppers. Malnutrition was common and many individuals suffered from hunger and dehydration.

6. Psychological Trauma: The combination of physical abuse, confinement, and witnessing the suffering and death of fellow captives caused severe psychological trauma among the enslaved. The trauma of the Middle Passage had lasting effects on those who survived.

8. Suicide and Resistance: Some enslaved Africans chose to resist their captors by refusing to eat, attempting suicide, or revolting. These acts of resistance were often met with brutal punishment.

According to Manning (1990), Africa's population was drastically reduced to 50% of its potential population growth due to slavery by the nineteenth century.

AFRICA'S POPULATION STAGNATES DURING THE TRANSATLANTIC SLAVE TRADE

	1600	1700	1800
Europe	111	125	203
Asia	339	436	635
Africa	**114**	**106**	**107**

(Population figures in the millions. World population by region

The table above clearly revealed that during the entire period of the slave trade, Africa's population did not increase while the people of other continents were increasing. Africa was the only continent that lost its population to slavery in this way. It was the greatest forced migration of a human population in history.

The loss of population due to slavery devastated the development of Africa. Those captured for slavery were young men and women and boys and girls in their prime. They were rooted from their place of origin without permission and were transported to the Caribbean, North and South America, Europe, and elsewhere for over 400 years. The slave trade also exaggerated the difference in ethnic fractionalisation between African ethnic groups, caused the breakdown of legal and political institutions, and made them unable to enforce good behaviour among citizens. Of all the evil that the slave trade caused to the African Continent, the greatest was the weakening of trust. Slavery in Africa over a long period created a culture of distrust, pervasive betrayal, an uncertain environment, violence, and warfare that had detrimental impacts on African societies' culture, social, and agricultural development. Slavery has affected the Africans' psychology and social fabric, especially in terms of violence and trust, to date.

The slave trade also increased the prevalence of polygamy (i. e. the practice of men having multiple wives). During the trans-Sahara trade, primarily females were captured and shipped to the Arabs for the sex trade, the sex ratio being about two females to one man. This led to the abuse, degradation of, and violence of women.

Removing so many youths from the population over many generations (a long period of 400 years) resulted in a huge reduction in the number of babies born because these demographics were of child-bearing age.

In addition, slavery prevented the remaining population from effectively engaging in agriculture. Violence in the form of raiding and kidnapping, rather than regular warfare, led to increased fear, uncertainty, and insecurity that deterred many farmers from going freely to their farm out of fear of being kidnapped. Labour also moved away from agriculture to more lucrative but brutal and disruptive activities such as war, kidnapping, or being intermediaries for European slave traders.

During the slave trade era, many civilian Africans developed a vigilant and fearful attitude toward any foreigner. With the heightened risk of slave raids by Arab or European slave traders in Western and Central Africa as well as Arab slave traders in East Africa, many civilian Africans switched to subsistence farming, foregoing any long-term planning.

CONTEMPORARY IMPACT AND ONGOING STRUGGLES:

Today, the African Diaspora is a global phenomenon with significant communities in North America, South America, the Caribbean, Europe, and beyond.

The African Diaspora in the modern era represents the global dispersion of people of African descent, particularly those who were forcibly taken from Africa during the transatlantic slave trade and their descendants. This diaspora has faced numerous struggles but has also achieved significant milestones and contributions to various aspects of society. Here are some key aspects of the African Diaspora in the modern era:

Struggles:

Slavery and Oppression: Enslaved Africans endured centuries of brutal and dehumanizing conditions during the transatlantic slave trade and the era of slavery in the Americas. This legacy of oppression left deep scars on African Diaspora communities.

Discrimination and Racism: Even after the abolition of slavery, African Diaspora communities faced pervasive racism and discrimination, including segregation, Jim Crow laws, and systemic inequalities in education, housing, and employment.

Civil Rights Movement: The 20th century witnessed the Civil Rights Movement in the United States, led by figures like Martin Luther King Jr., which fought for equal rights and an end to segregation. It marked a significant turning point in the struggle for racial justice.

Global Struggles Against Colonialism: In addition to struggles in the Americas, African Diaspora communities also played pivotal roles in the fight against colonialism and apartheid in Africa and the Caribbean.

Contemporary Challenges: Today, African Diaspora communities continue to face challenges such as racial profiling, mass incarceration, and disparities in healthcare and education. Issues like police brutality and racial inequality remain pressing concerns.

COMPARISON OF THE ENSLAVEMENT OF JEWS IN EGYPT AND THE AFRICAN SLAVE TRADE

While the enslavement of Jews in Egypt and the African slave trade were distinct historical events with unique circumstances, there are some similarities and parallels that can be drawn, particularly in terms of the experiences of enslaved people and the enduring impact on their respective communities. It's important to note that these similarities should not overshadow the differences and complexities of each historical event. Here are some key points of comparison:

1. Forced Labor and Oppression: Both the enslaved Jews in Egypt and African slaves during the transatlantic slave trade experienced forced labour and brutal oppression. They were subjected to gruelling physical work, harsh conditions, and mistreatment by their captors.

2. Loss of Freedom and Identity: Enslaved individuals in both contexts were stripped of their freedom and faced the loss of their cultural and familial identities. They were often forced to adopt the customs, beliefs, and languages of their oppressors.

3. Separation from Homeland: Enslaved Jews were separated from their ancestral homeland in Canaan for over 400 years, while African slaves were forcibly taken from their homelands in Africa for over 400 years. This separation from their places of origin created a profound sense of displacement and loss.

4. Resistance and Resilience: Enslaved people in both contexts demonstrated remarkable resilience and resistance. They found ways to preserve their cultural practices, traditions, and faith despite the challenges they faced.

5. Leadership and Liberation: Both narratives feature leaders who played crucial roles in the liberation of the enslaved population. In the Jewish narrative, it was Moses who led the Israelites out of Egypt. In African history, there were various leaders and movements, such as Nat Turner's rebellion and the Haitian Revolution, that sought to secure freedom.

6. Collective Memory and Cultural Preservation: Both the Jewish and African diaspora communities have maintained a strong collective memory of their histories of enslavement. They have preserved their cultural and religious traditions, passing them down through generations.

7. Impact on Future Generations: The experiences of enslavement had profound and lasting impacts on the descendants of both Jewish and African enslaved populations. These legacies continue to influence the cultural, social, and political landscapes of their respective communities.

8. Quest for Justice and Recognition: Both groups have advocated for justice, recognition, and reparations related to their histories of enslavement. Efforts to address the historical injustices have been ongoing.

While these similarities exist, it's essential to recognize that the contexts and details of the two historical events are distinct. The Jewish enslavement in Egypt occurred over 400 years, as recounted in the biblical narrative, in addition, the transatlantic slave trade also involved centuries of forced migration, labour, and exploitation. However, the specific cultural, religious, and regional contexts of the two groups are different.

Understanding these parallels can foster empathy and solidarity among diverse communities that have faced historical oppression. However, it's equally important to acknowledge and respect the unique experiences and narratives of each group.

LESSON LEARNT FROM THE BEHAVIOUR AND CONDUCT OF THE JEWS AFTER CROSSING THE RED SEA.

The biblical account of the crossing of the Red Sea is one of the most iconic events in the history of the Children of Israel. After their miraculous deliverance from slavery in Egypt, the Israelites embarked on a journey toward the Promised Land. This section explores the similarities and differences between the behaviour and conduct of the Children of Israel immediately after crossing the Red Sea and the behaviour and attitude of African nations post-independence. It's important to note that these are distinct historical and cultural contexts, but some parallels and contrasts can be drawn:

Similarities:

Initial Gratitude and Optimism: Just as the Children of Israel initially expressed gratitude and optimism after their liberation, many African nations displayed a sense of hope, unity, and optimism upon gaining independence from colonial powers. There was often a strong sense of national pride and a belief in a brighter future.

Challenges and Discontent: Both the Children of Israel in the wilderness and newly independent African nations faced significant challenges. The Israelites struggled with scarcity of resources while African nations grappled with the legacies of colonialism, including economic disparities, infrastructure challenges, and political instability. This led to moments of discontent and frustration.

Testing of Leadership: In both cases, there was a testing of leadership. Moses faced the challenge of guiding the Israelites through the wilderness while African leaders were tasked with nation-building and addressing complex post-colonial issues. Leadership decisions and responses to challenges had a profound impact on the trajectory of both groups.

Differences:

Nature of Challenges: While the challenges faced by the Children of Israel were often environmental and related to survival in the wilderness, African nations faced a wide range of challenges, including political fragmentation, ethnic tensions, economic disparities, and the need to establish functioning governance systems. These challenges were multifaceted and often required complex solutions.

Diversity of Nations: The Children of Israel were a single group with a shared history and destiny. In contrast, Africa is incredibly diverse, with numerous distinct nations, cultures, and histories. The post-independence experiences of African nations have varied significantly due to these differences.

Response to Challenges: While the Children of Israel's response to challenges included moments of disobedience, African nations have faced diverse responses to their challenges. Some nations have experienced political stability, economic growth, and social progress while others have struggled with corruption, conflict, and authoritarian rule.

External Factors: African nations' post-independence experiences have often been influenced by external factors, including global geopolitics, international aid, and foreign interference. These external factors have played a significant role in shaping the trajectory of African nations, which differs from the largely self-contained challenges faced by the Children of Israel in the wilderness.

Conclusion: While there are some similarities in terms of initial gratitude, challenges, and leadership testing, the behaviour and attitude of the Children of Israel after crossing the Red Sea and the post-independence experiences of African nations are fundamentally distinct due to the different historical, cultural, and geopolitical contexts. Understanding these differences and similarities can provide insights into the dynamics of nation-building, governance, and resilience in the face of challenges in different historical contexts.

CHAPTER 9
BABYLONIAN CONQUEST OF JERUSALEM

THE BABYLONIAN EXILE, also known as the Babylonian Captivity, was a defining moment in Jewish history that occurred in the 6th century BCE. It was a result of the conquest of the Kingdom of Judah and the city of Jerusalem by the Babylonian Empire.

The Babylonian Conquest of Jerusalem is a significant event in ancient history, particularly in the context of biblical narratives. It marked the fall of the Kingdom of Judah, the destruction of Jerusalem, and the exile of a portion of the Jewish population to Babylon. This event is documented in the Hebrew Bible, specifically in the Books of 2 Kings, 2 Chronicles, Jeremiah, and the Book of Lamentations.

Here's an overview of the Babylonian Conquest of Jerusalem. In the late 7th and early 6th centuries BCE, the Kingdom of Judah was under the rule of King Zedekiah. The region had been experiencing political instability and faced the looming threat of the Babylonian Empire, which was under the rule of King Nebuchadnezzar II.

Siege of Jerusalem (589-587 BCE): In 589 BCE, Nebuchadnezzar's forces laid siege to Jerusalem. The siege lasted for several years, leading to severe famine and suffering within the city's walls.

Destruction of Jerusalem (587/586 BCE): In 587/586 BCE, the Babylonians breached Jerusalem's walls and entered the city. They set fire to the First Temple (Solomon's Temple), destroying it completely. This event is known as the Destruction of the First Temple.

Exile to Babylon: Following the capture of Jerusalem, many of the city's residents were either killed or taken into captivity by the Babylonians. This period of exile, known as the Babylonian Captivity, marked a major turning point in Jewish history. The prophet Jeremiah had warned of the impending doom and called for submission to Babylonian rule as a means of survival.

The Babylonian Captivity lasted for 70 years, during which the exiled Jews maintained their religious and cultural identity, contributing to the development of Jewish traditions and writings, such as the Book of Ezekiel. During their exile, the Judeans faced the challenge of maintaining their religious and cultural identity in a foreign land. Religious leaders and prophets, such as Ezekiel and Daniel, played significant roles in providing spiritual guidance to the exiled community.

Religious Reflection and Adaptation: The experience of exile prompted theological reflection on the reasons for the catastrophe and the role of faith in times of adversity. It also led to adaptations in religious practices, such as the development of the synagogue as a place of communal worship and study.

The Return from Exile: After the fall of the Babylonian Empire to the Persians in 539 BCE, Cyrus the Great, the Persian king, issued a decree allowing the Jewish exiles to return to their homeland and rebuild the Temple in Jerusalem. This event is known as the Babylonian Exile and Return.

The Babylonian Conquest and the subsequent Babylonian Captivity had a profound impact on Jewish identity and religious traditions. It led to the preservation of the Hebrew Bible, the development of synagogue worship, and a strengthened sense of Jewish community.

The destruction of the First Temple and the subsequent construction of the Second Temple also played a significant role in shaping the religious practices of Judaism.

Cultural Adaptation: In Babylon, Jewish communities adapted to their surroundings while maintaining their distinctive religious practices. This adaptability and cultural resilience allowed Jewish identity to flourish despite the challenges of exile.

THE ROMAN DESTRUCTION OF JERUSALEM

The destruction of the Second Temple in 70 CE by the Roman Empire was a pivotal moment in Jewish history, marking the culmination of a series of conflicts between Jewish and Roman authorities. This event had profound and lasting consequences for the Jewish people, shaping their religious practices, beliefs, and diasporic existence.

Jewish-Roman Conflicts: Tensions between Jewish and Roman authorities had been escalating for years, fuelled by issues such as taxation, religious practices, and the desire for autonomy. These conflicts culminated in a full-scale Jewish revolt against Roman rule, resulting in the Roman siege and eventual destruction of Jerusalem.

The First Jewish-Roman War, also known as the Great Jewish Revolt, was a major conflict that took place from 66 to 73 CE in the Roman province of Judea. It was a significant event in Jewish history and had profound consequences for the Jewish population in Judea and the relationship between Jews and the Roman Empire.

Here is an overview of the First Jewish-Roman War. Judea had been under Roman rule since 6 CE, following the Roman conquest of Jerusalem and the incorporation of the region into the Roman Empire. Tensions had been building between the Jewish population and the Roman authorities due to various factors, including religious differences, taxation, and Roman interference in Jewish affairs.

Outbreak of the Revolt (66 CE): The immediate trigger for the revolt was a dispute over the Roman procurator Gessius Florus's confiscation of silver from the Second Temple in Jerusalem. The Jewish population of Jerusalem protested this act, which lead to a violent clash with Roman forces.

Leadership and Early Successes: The Jewish revolt was initially led by a coalition of leaders, including Eleazar ben Simon and Menahem, who seized control of Jerusalem. The Romans suffered initial setbacks as Jewish rebels captured several Roman garrisons in Judea.

Roman Response: The Roman Emperor Nero dispatched General Vespasian to crush the revolt. Vespasian's son, Titus, played a prominent role in the Roman campaign. Roman legions began besieging Jewish strongholds, including Jerusalem.

Siege and Destruction of Jerusalem (70 CE): The climax of the war came with the siege of Jerusalem, which began in 70 CE. The Jewish population suffered from famine and internal divisions. After a prolonged siege, the Romans breached the city's walls which resulted in intense fighting and the eventual capture of Jerusalem.

The Second Temple was destroyed by fire, marking a devastating loss for the Jewish people. This event is commemorated as the Ninth of Av (Tisha B'Av) in Jewish tradition.

Massacre and Exile: Following the capture of Jerusalem, the Romans massacred many Jewish residents and took others as slaves. The Arch of Titus in Rome commemorates this victory. The Jewish population faced widespread exile, contributing to the Jewish Diaspora.

Conclusion of the War (73 CE): While Jerusalem had fallen, pockets of Jewish resistance continued in other parts of Judea. The war officially came to an end in 73 CE when the last Jewish stronghold, the mountain fortress of Masada, fell to the Romans.

Legacy: The First Jewish-Roman War had a profound and lasting impact on Jewish history. It marked the end of Jewish sovereignty in Judea and the loss of the Second Temple. The destruction of the Second Temple transformed Jewish worship, emphasizing synagogue-based prayer and study. The memory of the war and the loss of Jerusalem and the Temple continued to shape Jewish identity and religious practice throughout the subsequent centuries.

The Diaspora: The destruction of the Second Temple forced many Jews into exile, contributing to the growth of Jewish diaspora communities across the Roman Empire and beyond. The diaspora became a defining aspect of Jewish existence with Jews dispersed throughout the world.

Religious Transformation: The loss of the Second Temple necessitated a transformation of Jewish religious practices. Rabbinic Judaism emerged as a dominant religious and intellectual movement: it emphasises Torah study, synagogue worship, and ethical living.

Diaspora Communities and Cultural Contributions: Jewish diaspora communities, established in various regions, adapted to local cultures while preserving their Jewish identity and traditions. These communities contributed to the cultural and intellectual life of their host societies.

Economic and Intellectual Contributions: Jews in the diaspora engaged in various professions, including trade, finance, and scholarship. Jewish scholars and thinkers in diaspora communities made significant intellectual and cultural contributions to their host societies.

Jewish communities established themselves in major urban centres across the Roman Empire, including Rome, Alexandria, and Antioch. These communities became hubs of Jewish life, scholarship, and cultural exchange. This process of adaptation and integration varied across regions and over time.

The Jewish dispersion extended beyond the Roman Empire to regions such as Persia, India, and later, Europe and North Africa. Jewish communities in these regions developed unique traditions and cultural expressions.

THE JEWISH EXPULSION FROM IBERIA: A HISTORICAL TRAGEDY

The Jewish expulsion from Iberia, a pivotal event in Jewish history, unfolded during a tumultuous period of religious and political upheaval. Also known as the Sephardic Diaspora, this expulsion had profound consequences for the Jewish communities that had thrived in the Iberian Peninsula for centuries. This section delves into the circumstances leading to the expulsion, its impact on Jewish life, and the enduring legacy of Sephardic Jews worldwide.

Historical Background: The Iberian Peninsula, comprising modern-day Spain and Portugal, was home to a flourishing Jewish community for centuries. Jewish settlement in the region dates back to Roman times and by the medieval period, Jews played prominent roles in various aspects of society.

The Reconquista and Religious Tensions: The Reconquista, a long period of Christian military campaigns, aimed to recapture the Iberian Peninsula from Muslim rule. As Christian kingdoms expanded their territories, religious tensions escalated.

The Christian Reconquista often subjected Jews to periods of instability and violence, including forced conversions to Christianity, known as "conversos" or "New Christians."

The Spanish Inquisition: The establishment of the Spanish Inquisition in 1478 under Ferdinand and Isabella intensified the persecution of Jews and conversos. The Inquisition targeted those suspected of secretly practicing Judaism or adhering to their ancestral faith.

Many Jews and conversos faced trials, imprisonment, torture, and execution. The Inquisition further eroded the religious and cultural identity of Sephardic Jews.

The Edict of Expulsion: On March 31, 1492, King Ferdinand II of Aragon and Queen Isabella I of Castile issued the Alhambra Decree, also known as the Edict of Expulsion. This decree mandated the expulsion of all Jews from Spanish territory.

Sephardic Jews were given a choice: convert to Christianity, leave the country, or face execution. As a result, hundreds of thousands of Jews fled Spain, leaving behind their homes, possessions, and rich cultural heritage.

Impact on Jewish Life: The expulsion had a profound impact on Sephardic Jews. Many exiles settled in North Africa, the Ottoman Empire, the Netherlands, and the Americas, contributing to the spread of the Sephardic culture and traditions worldwide.

Sephardic Jews faced the challenge of preserving their Jewish identity while adapting to new environments and often facing discrimination.

Enduring Legacy: The Sephardic Diaspora has left a lasting legacy on Jewish culture, language, and traditions. Ladino, a Judeo-Spanish language, and Sephardic customs continue to be cherished by Sephardic communities worldwide.

Sephardic Diaspora: The Sephardic diaspora resulted in the establishment of Sephardic communities in diverse regions. These communities brought with them their distinct customs, traditions, and language, known as Ladino (Judeo-Spanish).

Ladino Language: Ladino, a Judeo-Spanish language, developed as a means of communication among Sephardic Jews in their new diaspora homes. It is a language that combines Spanish with Hebrew, Arabic, Turkish, and other influences. Sephardic literature and music in Ladino remain significant cultural expressions.

Religious Traditions: Sephardic Jews maintained their distinct religious practices and liturgy. Their religious traditions, including music and liturgical poetry (piyyutim), differ from those of Ashkenazi Jews.

In conclusion, the Jewish expulsion from Iberia stands as a tragic chapter in the history of Jewish persecution and forced migration. Yet, it also reveals the resilience of Sephardic Jews who, despite being uprooted from their ancestral homeland, managed to preserve their cultural heritage and contribute significantly to the global tapestry of Jewish life. The Sephardic Diaspora underscores the enduring strength of identity and the ability of communities to flourish even in the face of adversity.

CHAPTER 10
HISTORY OF THE JEWS IN AFRICA

Proportion of Jewish population, 2005

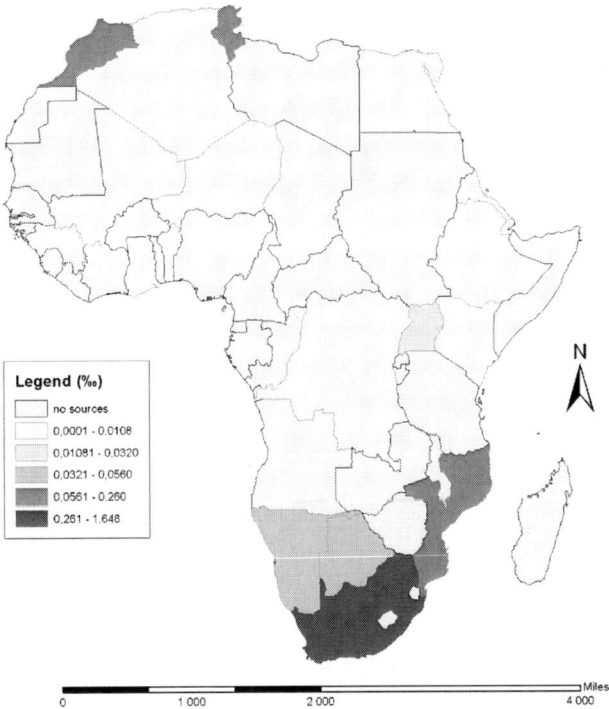

Legend (‰)

no sources
0,0001 - 0.0108
0,01081 - 0.0320
0,0321 - 0.0560
0,0561 - 0.260
0,261 - 1.648

Source: Wikipedia.com

THE HISTORY of Jews in Africa is a fascinating and multifaceted tale that spans over millennia, encompassing diverse regions, cultures, and interactions. The presence of Jewish communities in Africa dates to ancient times and their history is marked by contributions, interactions, and challenges within the continent's rich tapestry of cultures. This chapter provides an overview of the history of Jews in Africa, highlighting key moments, regions, and dynamics.

The presence of Jews in Africa predates the common era. Historical accounts suggest that Jewish traders, merchants, and settlers established communities along the North African coast, particularly in regions such as Egypt, Tunisia, and Morocco. These communities often engaged in trade and cultural exchange with indigenous peoples and contributed to the multicultural fabric of the region.

JEWS IN NORTH AFRICA

The earliest record of Jews in Egypt dates back to the Hellenistic period after the conquest of Alexander the Great. Jewish immigrants settled in Alexandria, one of the largest and most cosmopolitan cities in the ancient world.

Alexandria's Jewish community grew rapidly and played a vital role in the city's cultural and intellectual life. The translation of the Hebrew Bible into Greek, known as the Septuagint, is believed to have occurred in Alexandria during this time, called the Ptolemaic era, which began when Alexander the Great defeated the Persians in Egypt in 332 BCE. After his death in 323 BCE, his generals divided up his empire and Ptolemy took Egypt and proclaimed himself king in 305 BCE. During this period, Jews in Egypt enjoyed relative prosperity and cultural exchanges with the Hellenistic and Egyptian communities. The city of Alexandria became a significant center of Jewish life and scholarship, fostering cultural and intellectual interactions between Jewish, Greek, and Egyptian traditions.

With the Roman conquest of Egypt in 30 BCE, the status of Jews in Egypt fluctuated. At times, they faced discriminatory laws and measures, while at other times, they enjoyed periods of relative tolerance.

Under Roman and later Byzantine rule, the Jewish community in Alexandria continued to thrive and contribute to the region's intellectual and economic life.

Medieval and Islamic Egypt:

The Arab-Muslim conquest of Egypt in the 7th century CE ushered in a new era for Jews in Egypt. They were granted dhimmi (protected minority) status under Islamic law. As a result, Jewish communities spread across various regions of Egypt, including Cairo, Fustat, and Alexandria. Jews engaged in trade, crafts, and scholarship and made significant contributions to Egyptian society. In regions such as Morocco and Algeria, Jewish communities coexisted with Berber populations. These communities often adopted elements of local Berber culture while maintaining their Jewish identity.

The famed Jewish philosopher and scholar Maimonides (Rambam) was born in Cordoba, Spain, and later lived in Fustat, where he wrote many of his influential works.

Ottoman Period:

During the Ottoman Empire's rule, North Africa remained a diverse and dynamic region for Jewish communities. Cities like Tunis, Algiers, and Tripoli had significant Jewish populations engaged in trade, commerce, and crafts. Egypt became part of the Ottoman Empire in the early 16th century. Under Ottoman rule, Jews continued to live in various parts of Egypt, including Cairo.

The Jewish community played a role in trade, finance, and other economic activities, contributing to the country's prosperity.

Modern Era and Exodus:

The 19th and early 20th centuries saw a significant growth in the Jewish population in Egypt, particularly in Cairo and Alexandria. Jews were active in various professions, including law, medicine, and journalism.

However, political tensions and the Arab-Israeli conflict in the mid-20th century led to increased anti-Semitic sentiments and discrimination.

The exodus of most of Egypt's Jewish population took place in the mid-20th century, following the establishment of the State of Israel in 1948 and subsequent political changes in Egypt. The majority of Egyptian Jews left the country and today, only a tiny Jewish community remains.

Legacy and Heritage:

Despite the decline of the Jewish community in Egypt, their historical legacy endures. Ancient synagogues, Jewish cemeteries, and cultural artifacts bear witness to the rich Jewish heritage in the country. The story of Jews in Egypt is a testament to their resilience, contributions to Egyptian society, and the complexities of their historical interactions with various ruling powers.

Today, while the size of Jewish communities in North Africa is much smaller than in previous centuries, there are still Jewish communities in countries like Morocco, Tunisia, and Algeria. These communities continue to play roles in their respective countries and contribute to cultural diversity.

In conclusion, the history of Jews in North Africa is a multifaceted narrative that spans thousands of years and reflects the ebb and flow of Jewish life in the region. It reflects the long-standing presence of Jews in the region, their interactions with various cultures and civilizations, and their contributions to the social, economic, and intellectual life of North Africa

ISLAMIC RULE AND COEXISTENCE

With the spread of Islam across North Africa, Jewish communities often found themselves under Islamic rule. Despite differences in religious beliefs, Jewish communities often experienced periods of relative tolerance and coexistence with their Muslim neighbors, with instances of Jewish contributions to literature, philosophy, and trade.

This era was marked by a variety of experiences, including periods of relative tolerance, intellectual exchange, and coexistence, as well as episodes of discrimination and persecution. Here are some key aspects of Islamic rule and coexistence with Jewish communities in North Africa:

1. **Dhimmi Status:** Under Islamic rule, Jews were typically classified as dhimmis, a protected minority. This status afforded them certain rights and protections but also imposed certain restrictions. Dhimmis were required to pay a special tax (jizya) and adhere to specific regulations governing their religious practices and social status.
2. **Religious Freedom:** Despite the dhimmi status, Islamic societies generally allowed religious freedom for Jews. Jewish communities were allowed to practice their religion, maintain synagogues, and engage in religious scholarship.
3. **Economic and Cultural Contributions:** Jewish communities in North Africa played significant roles in the economic and cultural life of the region. They were often involved in trade, crafts, and finance and thus contributed to the prosperity of their host societies.

4. **Cultural Exchange:** Under Islamic rule, there was often a rich cultural exchange between Jewish and Muslim communities. This exchange influenced various fields, including literature, philosophy, and science. Jewish scholars in North Africa made important contributions to Islamic intellectual traditions.

5. **Golden Age of Jewish Scholarship:** The medieval period in North Africa witnessed a flourishing of Jewish scholarship, with renowned Jewish philosophers, theologians, and scholars like Maimonides (Rambam) emerging in places like Fustat (Cairo). These scholars engaged in philosophical dialogues with Islamic thought.

6. **Syncretism and Cultural Synthesis:** The coexistence of Jewish and Islamic cultures sometimes led to syncretism, where elements of both traditions influenced each other. This can be seen in aspects of language, cuisine, and even religious practices.

7. **Intermarriage and Social Interaction:** In some periods and regions, there were instances of intermarriage and social interaction between Jewish and Muslim communities. These interactions contributed to cultural exchange and social cohesion.

8. **Periods of Persecution:** While there were periods of tolerance and coexistence, Jewish communities in North Africa also faced episodes of discrimination and persecution. These challenges could be influenced by political changes, economic factors, or religious tensions.

9. **Decline and Emigration:** In the modern era, the Jewish communities in North Africa began to decline, partly due to factors like the founding of the State of Israel and increased anti-Semitic sentiments. Many Jews emigrated from North Africa to Israel and other countries.

10. **Cultural Legacy:** The history of Jewish-Muslim coexistence in North Africa has left a lasting cultural and historical legacy. Today, the region bears the marks of this

rich interplay in its architecture, cuisine, music, and intellectual heritage.

In summary, the era of Islamic rule in North Africa witnessed a complex interplay of coexistence, cultural exchange, and challenges for Jewish communities. It was a period in which Jewish communities made significant contributions to the region's intellectual and cultural life while navigating the complexities of living as a minority under Islamic governance. This history underscores the enduring importance of intercultural dialogue and understanding in our diverse world.

CONTEMPORARY AFRICAN JEWISH COMMUNITIES:

While the majority of Jewish communities have traditionally been associated with North Africa, there have been notable Jewish communities in various Sub-Saharan African regions. Here is an overview of the history of Jews in Sub-Saharan Africa:

Ethiopia - Beta Israel (Ethiopian Jews): The Beta Israel, often referred to as Ethiopian Jews, are one of the most well-known Jewish communities in Sub-Saharan Africa. They trace their origins back to ancient times and have a unique religious tradition. Beta Israel have lived in different regions of Ethiopia, primarily in the northern highlands. Their religious practices and customs reflect a distinctive form of Judaism influenced by their isolation from other Jewish communities.

In the late 20th century, many Beta Israel members emigrated to Israel as part of large-scale rescue and immigration operations.

South Africa: South Africa has had a small but significant Jewish community since the late 19th century. Jewish immigrants, primarily of Ashkenazi (Eastern European) origin, played roles in commerce, industry, and politics. Some prominent anti-apartheid activists, such as Joe Slovo and Ruth First, were Jewish. The South

African Jewish community maintains its distinct identity while engaging in interfaith and intercultural dialogues.

Nigeria - Igbo Jews: In southeastern Nigeria, there is a community known as the Igbo Jews or the Jews of Nigeria. They claim descent from the biblical Israelites and adhere to Jewish customs and practices.

The Igbo Jews emerged in the 20th century and embraced Judaism as their faith. They have formed synagogues and some have pursued formal conversion to Judaism. This community, though small, has drawn attention for its unique blend of Jewish and Igbo cultural elements.

Ghana - House of Israel: In Ghana, there is a community known as the House of Israel. Members claim to be of Jewish descent and practice a form of Judaism influenced by their interpretation of the Hebrew Bible. The House of Israel has synagogues and follows certain Jewish rituals. The community is relatively small but has garnered interest from scholars and researchers.

Other Communities: In various other Sub-Saharan African countries, there are smaller Jewish communities or groups that identify with Judaism to varying degrees. These communities often have unique and diverse histories and practices.

It's important to note that the Jewish communities in Sub-Saharan Africa are not monolithic and their connections to mainstream Judaism vary. Additionally, Jewish identity and practice can be influenced by a range of factors, including historical migrations, local customs, and religious syncretism.

In conclusion, the history of Jews in Africa is a complex and diverse narrative, encompassing a wide range of experiences and interactions. From ancient settlements to diverse diaspora communities, Jews in Africa have contributed to the cultural, economic, and intellectual development of the continent. Their interactions with indigenous cultures, as well as with other religious and ethnic groups, have left an indelible mark on the African narrative, showcasing the enduring power of diversity and cultural exchange. From ancient settlements in North Africa to contemporary communities in South Africa, Ethiopia, and Nigeria, African Jews have made their mark on the continent's cultural, intellectual, and social tapestry. Their history serves as a testament to the enduring power of cultural identity, resilience in the face of challenges, and the potential for diverse communities to coexist and contribute to the rich mosaic of African life.

THE JEWISH UGANDA PROJECT

The Jewish Uganda Project, also known as the Uganda Scheme, is a lesser known but significant episode in Jewish history. Proposed by the British government in the early 20th century, it aimed to offer a homeland for Jewish refugees in East Africa, specifically in what is now Uganda. This section explores the origins, motivations, and outcomes of the Jewish Uganda Project and its impact on the broader Zionist movement.

The Context of Persecution: The late 19th and early 20th centuries witnessed growing anti-Semitism in Europe, particularly in Eastern Europe, where pogroms and discriminatory policies left Jewish communities vulnerable.

Theodor Herzl, the founder of modern political Zionism, was deeply concerned about the plight of persecuted Jews and sought a practical solution to the "Jewish Question."

The Uganda Offer: In 1903, the British government, under the leadership of Joseph Chamberlain, suggested the establishment of a Jewish homeland in British East Africa, specifically in Uganda. This offer was met with mixed reactions within the Zionist movement.

Herzl, while initially open to the Uganda offer, faced opposition from within the Zionist movement, particularly from those who believed that the project deviated from the core goal of a Jewish homeland in Palestine. The proposal led to heated debates and divisions among Zionists, with some fearing that acceptance of a homeland outside of Palestine would undermine the Zionist cause. The death of Theodor Herzl in 1904 significantly altered the course of the Uganda debate as he had been the most prominent advocate of the project.

At the 6th Zionist Congress in 1903, the majority of delegates rejected the Uganda proposal, reaffirming their commitment to establishing a Jewish homeland in Palestine.

Conclusion: The Jewish Uganda Project remains a complex and controversial chapter in Jewish history. While it ultimately was rejected by the Zionist movement, it highlighted the urgency of finding a safe haven for persecuted Jews during a period of increasing anti-Semitic violence. The project's rejection led to a reinvigorated commitment to the establishment of Israel in Palestine, but it also left questions about the potential for alternative Jewish homelands. In retrospect, the Uganda debate underscores the challenging decisions made by Jewish leaders at a pivotal moment in their history as they navigated the tensions between practical solutions and a deeply ingrained vision of a homeland in historic Palestine.

CHAPTER 11
THE COLONISATION OF AFRICA

"Evangelize the niggers so that they stay forever in submission to the white colonialists and never revolt against the restraints they are undergoing. Recite daily – 'happy are those who are weeping because the kingdom of God is for them.' Convert always the blacks by using the whip. Keep their women in nine months of submission to work freely for us. Force them to pay you in a sign of recognition – goats, chickens or eggs – every time you visit their villages. And make sure that niggers never become rich. Sing every day that the rich can't enter heaven. Make them pay tax each week at Sunday mass. Use the money supposed for the poor, to build flourishing business centres. Institute a confessional system, which allows you to be good detectives denouncing any black with a different consciousness, contrary to the decision-maker. Teach the niggers to forget their heroes and to adore only ours. Never present a chair to a black that comes to visit you. Don't give him more than one cigarette. Never invite him for dinner even if he gives you a chicken every time you arrive at his house."

KING LEOPOLD II (BELGIAN 1876)

PRIOR TO THE end of the 17th century, mosquitoes made Africa impenetrable to the Europeans and barely one in ten

European explorers that ventured into Africa survived malaria and yellow fever.

Below are a few factors that made African colonialism possible:

The discovery of quinine: Before the division of Africa, Europeans established modest commercial ports along its beaches. They only did business near the shore because of malaria and other diseases. Barely one in ten European explorers to Africa survived malaria and yellow fever. Thus, Europe nicknamed interior Africa "White Man's Grave." However, the discovery of quinine as a malaria remedy made Europeans explore hinterland Africa further.

Innovation: The invention of the steam engine and iron-hulled boats allowed Europeans to explore the continent's interior waterways, discover minerals, and export large goods from Africa inland to Europe.

Explorers, traders, and missionaries were all accomplices in the colonisation of Africa. Exploration, trade, and evangelising often shaded each other and were frequently entangled with military force and the establishment of colonial rule. Traders carried European technologies of warfare and production as well as goods while missionaries often advocated European social organization, education, and religious beliefs. All these profoundly alter the traditional patterns of African society.

"When the missionaries arrived, the Africans had the land, and the missionaries had the Bible." They taught us how to pray with our eyes closed. When we opened them, they had the land, and we had the Bible".

JOMO KENYATTA, THE FOUNDING FATHER AND FIRST PRESIDENT OF KENYA.

End of Slave Trade: Slavery ended in Europe, leaving a void that businesspeople rushed to fill. So, when explorers reported finding raw minerals on the continent, European businesspeople saw another opportunity to exploit black people.

During the early nineteen century, there were many tensions, decades-long wars, and rivalry between European countries. Colonization was a ploy used by European nations to distract themselves from battling each other in Europe. In 1871, the king of Belgium decided that Belgium should have a colony, looked at the world map, and noticed that Africa was weak and available.

King Leopold II of Belgium is a controversial figure in the history of the Democratic Republic of Congo (DRC). During his reign from 1865 to 1909, Leopold was responsible for some of the most brutal atrocities in the history of European colonialism in Africa, resulting in the deaths of over 10 million of Congolese people.

Presenting himself as a philanthropist eager to bring the benefits of Christianity, Western civilization, and commerce to African natives.

King Leopold II Source www.bbc.co.uk

King Leopold II of Belgium set up the International African Association in 1876 and sent explorers like Henry Morton Stanley to go and research inland Africa and open up the rainforest of Africa to the king's agents. Officially, this was supposed to be a kind of international philanthropic enterprise in which the "benevolent" king would shower African natives with the blessings of Christianity and steam engines. For five years, they travelled up and down the immense waterways of the Congo River basin. These explorers discovered that the continent had abundant natural resources, including gold, copper, rubber, palm oil, diamonds, etc. The discovery brought lots of attention to the African continent. European countries began to rush to Africa to gain control of huge parts of land that would give them access to gold and riches. Soon other European nations joined and almost all of Africa was colonized by European empires. Europe's imperialists used the Berlin Treaty of February 26, 1885 to divide Africa into "Portugal, British, German, Italian, Spanish, French, and Belgian Africa."

British Prime Minister Lord Salisbury duly captured the arbitrariness of the partitioning exercise. He said:

> *"We have been engaged in drawing lines upon maps of a continent where no white man's feet have ever trod. We have been giving away to ourselves mountains and rivers and lakes, only hindered by the small impediment that we never knew exactly where the mountains and rivers and lakes were."*

BRITISH PRIME MINISTER LORD SALISBURY

King Leopold then embarked on an ultimately successful effort to make a vast fortune from his new possession. Initially, he was most interested in ivory, a material that was greatly valued in the days before plastics because it could be carved into a great variety of shapes—statuettes, jewellery, piano keys, false teeth, and more.

By the early 1890s, a worldwide rubber boom was under way, kicked off by the invention of the inflatable bicycle tire. Leopold sent his 19,000-man private army, the Force Publique, to march into villages and hold the women hostage while forcing the men to scatter into the rainforest and gather a monthly quota of wild rubber. As the price of rubber soared, the quotas increased, and as vines near a village were drained dry, men desperate to free their wives and daughters would have to walk days or weeks to find new vines to tap. Individuals who failed to meet rubber quotas faced severe punishment, including death, taking family members hostage, amputation, and even burning entire villages to the ground.

EXECUTION OF SLAVES BY THE WAKUTI, NEAR EQUATOR STATION.

An illustration from HM Stanley's "The Congo and the founding of its free state; a story of work and exploration (1885)." A father stares at the hand and foot of his five-year-old daughter, severed as a punishment for having harvested too little rubber. May 1904,

As a result, 10 million people were killed under the brutal rule of King Leopold II. The international response to the cruel treatment of Africans forced King Leopold II to make the Congo Free State a colony of Belgium. It was then known as the Belgian Congo until it gained its independence in 1960 and became the Democratic Republic of Congo.

Italian versus Ethiopia

Contrary to popular belief, European colonisation of Africa was not an easy task. The coloniser and the colonised never had a loving or subservient relationship. All colonisers used violence and force to conquer the Africans.

The greatest humiliation suffered by a European state in the quest for empire was the Italians in Ethiopia. In late nineteenth-century Europe, Europeans universally despised Africans as backward and uncivilised. Italy had already conquered the horn of Africa and concluded a treaty with Menelik II, the Emperor of Ethiopia, in 1889. Unfortunately, the treaty broke down due to language misinterpretation in Italian and Amharic. In 1894, the Italians began military action. 15,000 Italian troops advanced in three columns, but they soon became separated and lost because the Italians did not have proper maps. They were met by nearly 100,000 Ethiopian troops, raised under the feudal system, supplied with modern rifles, and aided by 42 Russian field guns specially adapted for mountain terrain. Ethiopian cavalry slaughtered over 7,000 Italian soldiers and took 3,000 prisoners. This led to the resignation of Italian Prime Minister Crispi and exposed Italy to universal ridicule.

German colonialism

Namibia was populated by nomadic livestock herders from the Herero and Nama tribes. European arrival threatened their nomads' livelihood by an epidemic of a lethal cattle illness, Rinderpest, imported by Europeans towards the end of the 1890s. In the early 1900s, the colonial government's quick land grab led to the assault on German farmers. This offended Kaiser Wilhelm II, who feared being humiliated as Italy had been in Ethiopia in 1896. He sent 14,000 German soldiers from Berlin with the mandate that 'Any Herero discovered within the German claimed boundary, with or without a rifle or livestock, shall be executed.' The Namibians caught in the crossfire were murdered or hung.

The Germans then captured the rest of the tribe, chiefly women and children, along with Nama tribal members, and imprisoned them in "concentration camps" (the first official German use of this term). Those that survived were skeletons. The camps also became research locations for anthropologist Eugen Fischer, who became a key 'racial hygienist' during the Third Reich. The conflict decreased the Herero population from 85,000 to 15,000, while up to half of 20,000 Nama were killed.

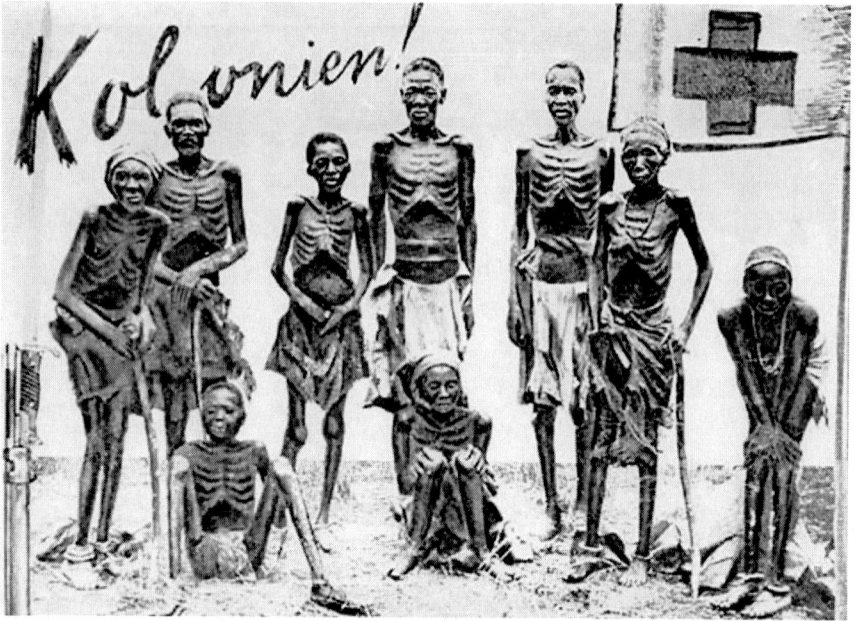

In 1907, the Herero tribe died of starvation at the hands of German. Most African European colonies saw daily violence, including public beatings of Africans.

British colonialism

The British empire was vast and varied, making generalisation impossible. In British settler colonies, like in German colonies, there was frequent and sometimes fatal violence, but by settlers rather than the colonial military. The British army devastated and burned down Benin city in Nigeria and Kumasi Palace in Ghana and plundered thousands of artefacts. Royal Navy detachment bombed and machine-gunned Zanzibar's harbour, killing 500 people.

When British immigrants first arrived in Kenya in 1902, they hoped to establish an agricultural colony that would assist funding other East African imperial initiatives. The British government then evicted Kenyan individuals whose relatives had lived there for a thousand years, with or without compensation, and put them in reserves. These reserves rapidly became overcrowded and overtaxed the marginal areas they were sited on. The Kikuyu, deprived of their land and rights, were pushed into rural ghettos and started mobilising. They went by the name of Kenya Land and Freedom Army (KLFA) oath-takers but were dubbed by the British authorities as Mau Mau

In the summer of 1955, Winston Churchill ordered an unending campaign. The British erected a network of detention camps around the province for interrogation. One day in Nairobi, the British detained 130,000 males and deported another 170,000 women and children to the camps. The suspects were beaten to gather evidence. A British soldier's preferred interrogation tactic was to hold a subject upside down in a pail of water and force sand into his rectum. Men were raped with knives, snakes, and scorpions, while women were gang-raped or had their breasts damaged with pliers. Thousands of Kikuyu were malnourished, beaten, and tortured to death in concentration camps, and in some instances, most children died.

Francophone countries

Interestingly, France's hold on Africa remains strong among all the colonisers. African French (French: français africain) is a collective term for the 158 million Africans who speak French as a primary or secondary language. The French did not want to give up their African territories during and after independence and thought their colonies should not profit from their development efforts. To get their message across to other French colonies, the French destroyed whatever they could in Guinea when the president of this African country tried to liberate itself from France. They set fire to food, livestock, houses, and literature. These heinous acts were meant to destabilise Guinea's new independence and staged coups against elected presidents of other colonies seeking independence.

As a result, other Francophone African nations were forced to sign cooperation pacts to maintain their links with France. Affaires franco-coloniales allowed France to develop a system of collaboration and conformity that lasted long after independence.

The obligations that France subjected some ex-French colonies under the colonial pact include:

- Paying for the infrastructure France built during colonisation – colonial tax.
- Keeping 50 % of their foreign reserves in the French Treasury - 14 African countries have been doing this for years. Interestingly, these countries can only access 15 % of their reserves each year. If they need more, they have to borrow it.
- France has the first right to purchase any natural resources discovered in their country.
- French companies have dibs on all government procurement bids

- Senior military officers are trained in France, so the personnel can be used to stage a coup.
- France has the right to deploy its military in the African countries
- African countries must make French the official language and the education language.
- Using the French colonial currency.
- Former colonies must send a reserve report to France.
- Ex-colonies cannot enter military alliances with other countries without approval from France.
- Ex-colonies are required to join forces with France during war or global crises.

This agreement, which dates back to the 1960s, benefited French banks and the state but denied African nations income and progress. Since the monetary system was implemented, African governments have lost $500 billion, robbing Africans of wealth and development, and France would do everything to preserve it.

France controls the money supply, financial laws, banking operations, and budgetary and economic policies; Francophone nations have stayed impoverished. In Côte d'Ivoire, French companies own and control all the major utilities: water, electricity, telephone, transport, ports, and major banks.

This unchecked neo-colonial policy could not have succeeded if not for the African governing elites who relied on France's political, technical, military, and economic support. Any leader who disobeys France's will or tries to leave the French economic zone must deal with the consequences of political, financial, and military pressure. For instance, in January 1963, President Silvanus Olympia of Togo was assassinated three days before issuing a new currency. Other notable leaders include David Dacko, President of the Central African Republic; Thomas Isidore Nol Sankara, President of Burkina Faso; and Maka Modibo Keita, Prime Minister of Mali. All were assassinated or overthrown in coups due to their quest for monetary independence. France has intervened militarily 40 times across Africa since the 1960s. Though the French monetary system is illegal, African countries cannot afford to sue. The world community is aware of this deception but does nothing.

THE CONSEQUENCES OF COLONISATION

Below are the few consequences of the partitioning of Africa by Europe.

Civil Wars: As a result of the partition and colonisation, in most African nations, a large portion of the population (approximately 40–45%) was placed together along national borders where there was no commonality. Some old adversaries were reunited. Europe drew the split for economic reasons and not because they understood or cared about any of these ethnic groups or where their borders began or ended. Some ethnic groups are split between two or more nations. For example, the Maasai were divided between Kenya (62%), Tanzania (38%) and Tanzania (62%), whereas the Anyi was split between Ghana (58%) and Ivory Coast (42%). The Malinke ethnic group has the highest index score, followed by the Ndembu (Angola, Zaire, and Zambia) and the Nuke (Angola, Namibia, Zambia, and Botswana).

Lumping together ethnic groups with long historical hatred led to above-average ethnic strife in Sub-Saharan Africa. To understand the implication of mixing ethnic groups arbitrarily, we only need to consider the Russia and Ukraine war and the fight over the Donbas region. Russia claimed the region is part of the Russian Federation because the people speak Russian. And as a result, war broke out in Europe after 70 years of peace.

The European partition has caused more war and warfare in Africa than the media made us understand. The frequency and severity of these disagreements have reduced motivation and made it difficult to adapt and develop institutions. According to an empirical study based on 43,000 documented disputes in Africa from 1969 to 2000, the ethnic map constructed by Europeans was highly detrimental to peace.

SIMILARITIES BETWEEN JEWISH COLONIZATION BY ROME AND AFRICAN COLONIZATION BY EUROPE

The history of colonization is marked by the expansion of powerful empires and nations into territories inhabited by other peoples. While the Jewish colonization by Rome and the European colonization of Africa occurred in different time periods and contexts, there are significant similarities in their underlying dynamics, impacts, and consequences. This section explores these similarities, shedding light on the shared experiences of subjugation, cultural assimilation, and resistance that both Jewish and African populations faced during these colonial periods.

Imperial Expansion and Subjugation:

Jewish Colonization by Rome: The Jewish colonization by Rome began with the Roman conquest of Judea in the 1st century BCE. Rome imposed its rule over the Jewish population, leading to a loss of political autonomy and sovereignty.

African Colonization by Europe: European colonization of Africa, which reached its peak in the late 19th and early 20th centuries, involved the subjugation of numerous African societies under European imperial powers. Africans, like the Jews, experienced a loss of sovereignty and self-determination.

Cultural Assimilation:

Jewish Colonization by Rome: Under Roman rule, Jews faced pressure to assimilate into Roman culture, including adopting Roman religious practices and customs. The destruction of the Second Temple in 70 CE marked a turning point as it disrupted traditional Jewish religious life.

African Colonization by Europe: European colonial powers imposed their culture and language on African societies. African languages, traditions, and belief systems were marginalized or suppressed in favour of European norms, leading to a cultural transformation.

Economic Exploitation:

Jewish Colonization by Rome: Jews in Roman-occupied territories faced economic exploitation through taxation and tribute to the Roman Empire, which often resulted in economic hardship for Jewish communities.

African Colonization by Europe: European colonial powers exploited Africa's resources, including minerals, rubber, and agricultural products, to fuel their own economies. This economic exploitation led to the impoverishment of African nations.

Resistance and Revolt:

Jewish Colonization by Rome: Jewish resistance against Roman rule is well-documented, culminating in the Jewish-Roman Wars, including the First Jewish-Roman War (66-73 CE) and the Bar Kokhba Revolt (132-136 CE).

African Colonization by Europe: Africa witnessed numerous resistance movements and uprisings against colonial rule. These included armed rebellions, such as the Maji Maji Rebellion in German East Africa and the Mau Mau Uprising in Kenya, the destruction of the Benin Empire and Kumasi as well as non-violent resistance movements.

Impact on Identity and Legacy:

Jewish Colonization by Rome: The Jewish experience under Roman colonization contributed to the development of a strong Jewish identity and the preservation of Jewish religious traditions, even in diaspora.

African Colonization by Europe: European colonization significantly impacted African identities. It led to a complex legacy of cultural hybridity, where traditional African elements often coexist with elements of European culture.

In conclusion, while Jewish colonization by Rome and African colonization by Europe occurred in different historical and geographical contexts, there are striking similarities in their experiences of subjugation, cultural assimilation, economic exploitation, resistance, and the enduring impact on identity. Recognizing these parallels helps us understand the shared history of colonization and its lasting effects on both Jewish and African communities and highlights the resilience and determination of these populations in the face of adversity.

INFERIORITY COMPLEX DURING JEWISH AND BLACK SLAVERY

Numbers 11:4-6 in the Bible "Meanwhile, the rabble among them had a strong craving for other food, and again the Israelites wept and said, "Who will feed us meat? We remember the fish we ate freely in Egypt, along with the cucumbers, melons, leeks, onions, and garlic. But now our appetite is gone; there is nothing to see but this manna!"

The historical narratives of Jewish slavery in ancient Egypt and the transatlantic slave trade that ensnared millions of Africans have striking parallels. Beyond the physical horrors and injustices, both episodes of slavery left indelible marks on the psyches of the enslaved peoples. One significant aspect of this enduring impact was the development of an inferiority complex. This section explores the manifestation and consequences of the inferiority complex among Jews in biblical Egypt and black slaves during the transatlantic slave trade, shedding light on the psychological scars that persist to this day.

I. The Jewish Experience in Ancient Egypt

The biblical account of the Israelites' slavery in Egypt, as recorded in the Book of Numbers, offers insights into the emergence of an inferiority complex:

1. **Craving for Egypt:** The Israelites' exodus from Egypt was marked by their longing for the familiar, despite the harsh conditions of slavery. This sentiment reflects a sense of inadequacy and dependency cultivated during their bondage.
2. **Yearning for Egyptian Food:** The Israelites' reminiscence of Egyptian food, including fish, cucumbers, melons, leeks, onions, and garlic, underscores the influence of Egyptian culture and lifestyle on their identity. Their perceived inability to thrive without such comforts implies a diminished self-image.
3. **Complaints about Manna:** The Israelites' dissatisfaction with the divinely provided manna, which was meant to sustain them in the wilderness, highlights their struggle to adapt to freedom. This dissatisfaction can be seen as an expression of their lingering feelings of inferiority and dependency.

II. The African Experience in the Transatlantic Slave Trade

Similarly, the transatlantic slave trade left an enduring legacy of inferiority complex among black Africans:

1. **Cultural Erasure:** Enslaved Africans were forcibly stripped of their cultural identities, languages, and traditions. The imposition of European customs and values instilled a sense of cultural inferiority, as Africans were made to view their heritage as primitive or backward.

2. **Brutalization and Dehumanization:** The degrading treatment of black slaves, including physical abuse and the denial of basic human rights, reinforced the perception of being inherently inferior. The institution of slavery portrayed black Africans as subhuman, further undermining their self-worth.
3. **Internalization of Stereotypes:** Over time, many enslaved Africans internalized the negative stereotypes and biases propagated by their oppressors. They began to perceive themselves through the lens of these stereotypes, contributing to the development of an inferiority complex.

III. Consequences of the Inferiority Complex

The inferiority complex that emerged during Jewish and black slavery has had lasting consequences:

1. **Interpersonal Relationships:** Feelings of inferiority can manifest in interpersonal relationships, affecting self-esteem and interactions with others. Survivors of slavery often faced challenges in forming healthy relationships due to these deep-seated insecurities.
2. **Identity and Self-Worth:** The inferiority complex has influenced the identity and self-worth of descendants of both Jewish and black slaves. Overcoming this legacy of self-doubt and inadequacy has been a protracted struggle.
3. **Collective Memory:** These historical experiences have been embedded in the collective memory of Jewish and black communities. The inferiority complex continues to shape their cultural narratives, influencing their understanding of identity and heritage.

The impact of an inferiority complex, borne out of the experiences of Jewish slavery in ancient Egypt and the transatlantic slave trade, extends far beyond historical events. It persists as a psychological scar that affects the self-perception, identity, and collective memory of these communities. Recognizing the enduring legacy of this complex is a crucial step toward healing and empowerment for descendants of those who endured these traumas. It is a reminder that history's wounds, though deep, can be addressed with empathy, education, and a commitment to justice and equality

OVER-DEPENDENCY ON COLONISERS

The verse from the Book of 1 Samuel 13;9, "Not a blacksmith could be found in the whole land of Israel, because the Philistines had said, 'Otherwise the Hebrews will make swords or spears!'" serves as a poignant example of the impact of over-dependency on a community's autonomy and well-being. This verse provides a glimpse into the historical struggles of the Jewish people during the period of Philistine domination. Likewise, it parallels instances of over-dependency experienced by African colonized nations during the era of European colonialism. This section explores the repercussions of over-dependency on the Jewish community in ancient Israel and on colonized African nations, examining the historical contexts and lasting consequences.

I. Over-Dependency in Ancient Israel

During the period described in the Book of Samuel, the Philistines' strategic suppression of blacksmiths in Israel illustrates the consequences of over-dependency:

1. **Economic Dependency:** The Philistines recognized the pivotal role of blacksmiths in producing weapons and tools. By monopolizing blacksmithing, they ensured Israel's economic reliance on Philistine-controlled blacksmiths for essential tools and weapons.
2. **Technological Stagnation:** Israel's inability to access blacksmithing skills stifled technological advancement.

Over time, they became reliant on Philistine expertise, leading to a lack of innovation and self-sufficiency in crafting weapons and tools.

3. **Loss of Autonomy:** The Hebrews' dependency on the Philistines for their basic needs, particularly in defence, eroded their autonomy and self-determination. This over-dependency weakened their ability to resist external domination effectively.

II. Over-Dependency during Colonization

The impact of over-dependency during colonization was similarly profound, as colonized nations experienced various forms of dependency on their colonial rulers:

1. **Economic Exploitation:** Colonizers exploited the economies of their colonies, extracting valuable resources for their own benefit while hindering the development of local industries. This economic dependency perpetuated poverty and underdevelopment.

2. **Cultural Suppression:** Colonial powers often imposed their cultures, languages, and values on colonized populations, erasing indigenous identities and fostering dependency on the colonizers' ways of life.

3. **Political Subjugation:** Colonized nations were subjected to foreign governance and often had limited autonomy in political decision-making. Their dependency on colonial administrations left them vulnerable to lack of good leadership, exploitation and oppression.

III. Consequences of Over-Dependency

The consequences of over-dependency were significant for both ancient Israel and colonized nations:

1. **Loss of Autonomy:** Over-dependency invariably led to a loss of autonomy and self-determination. In both cases, the inability to meet essential needs independently resulted in subjugation to external forces.
2. **Stagnation and Underdevelopment:** Over time, both the Israelites and colonized nations suffered from stagnation and underdevelopment. The lack of self-sufficiency stifled progress and innovation in various fields.
3. **Cultural Erosion:** Cultural erosion was a common consequence of over-dependency. The imposition of foreign cultures and values often resulted in the loss of indigenous identities and traditions.

In conclusion, the verse from the Book of Samuel serves as a poignant reminder of the profound impact of over-dependency on communities and nations throughout history. Whether during the time of ancient Israel or the era of colonization, over-dependency led to the loss of autonomy, stagnation, cultural erosion, and economic exploitation. Recognizing the consequences of over-dependency is essential for understanding historical injustices and their enduring effects. It underscores the importance of striving for self-sufficiency, autonomy, and empowerment to break free from the chains of dependency and secure a brighter future.

THE LIMITATIONS OF UNPROVEN IDEOLOGY

1 Samuel 17:38-58 Then Saul gave David his own armour—a bronze helmet and a coat of mail. David put it on, strapped the sword over it, and took a step or two to see what it was like, for he had never worn such things before. "I can't go in these," he protested to Saul. "I'm not used to them." So, David took them off again. He picked up five smooth stones from a stream and put them into his shepherd's bag. Then, armed only with his shepherd's staff and sling, he started across the valley to fight the Philistine

The verses depicting the young David's rejection of Saul's armour in favour of his simple sling and stones is a powerful illustration of the limitations of unproven ideology. This episode from the Bible resonates with parallels from the era of colonization when indigenous populations often faced the imposition of foreign ideologies and practices. This section delves into the implications of unproven ideology during the time of ancient Israel and colonization, highlighting the challenges and consequences that arose from attempting to implement untested beliefs.

I. Unproven Ideology in Ancient Israel

1. **Saul's Armour and David's Rejection:** The story of David and Goliath showcases the conflict between traditional, unproven armour and David's reliance on his tried-and-true shepherd's tools. David's rejection of Saul's armour stems from his lack of familiarity with these untested weapons. His trust in his sling and stones reflects the limitations of unproven ideology in the face of practical, real-world challenges.
2. **The Power of Tradition:** David's decision to stick with his shepherd's tools underscores the power of tradition and the value of what is known and tested. Judges 20:16 "Among Benjamin's elite troops, 700 were left-handed, and each of them could sling a rock and hit a target within a hairsbreadth without missing." Unproven ideologies often fail to account for the nuances and complexities of real-life situations, making them ill-suited for practical application.

II. Unproven Ideology during Colonization

1. **Colonial Imposition of Ideology:** Colonial powers often imposed their ideologies, technologies, and practices on indigenous populations. These unproven ideologies were presented as superior and were expected to replace traditional customs and practices.
2. **Resistance and Preservation:** Colonized communities faced the challenge of preserving their traditional ways of life while navigating the pressures of colonialism. They often resisted the imposition of foreign ideologies, recognizing the limitations and impracticality of these unproven systems.

III. Consequences of Unproven Ideology

1. **Cultural Erosion:** Unproven ideologies, when forced upon indigenous populations, frequently led to the erosion of traditional cultures, languages, and practices. This cultural loss had lasting impacts on identity and heritage.
2. **Practical Ineffectiveness:** Unproven ideologies often proved impractical in the contexts of colonization and daily life. They failed to address the specific needs and challenges faced by colonized peoples and lead to inefficiencies and difficulties.
3. **Resistance and Adaptation:** Colonized communities, like David, often had to adapt and resist foreign ideologies to protect their way of life. This resistance highlighted the limitations and inadequacies of unproven systems.

In conclusion, the story of David's rejection of Saul's armour and the broader historical context of colonization illustrates the limitations of unproven ideology. Unproven beliefs and practices often fail when confronted with the complexities of the real world. They can lead to cultural erosion, impracticality, and resistance. Recognizing these limitations is essential in understanding the challenges faced by communities like the ancient Israelites and colonized nations. It emphasizes the importance of preserving traditional knowledge and practices while critically evaluating the feasibility of unproven ideologies before their implementation. Ultimately, history teaches us that relying on what is tried and true, rather than embracing untested beliefs, can be a path to resilience and success in the face of adversity.

REMEMBERING HOME

The verses from Psalm 137: 2-6 By the rivers of Babylon we sat and wept when we remembered Zion. There on the poplars we hung our harps, for there our captors asked us for songs, our tormentors demanded songs of joy; they said, "Sing us one of the songs of Zion!" How can we sing the songs of the Lord while in a foreign land? If I forget you, Jerusalem, may my right hand forget its skill. May my tongue cling to the roof of my mouth if I do not remember you".

These verses serve as a poignant reminder of the enduring connection between diaspora communities and their ancestral homelands. This section explores the profound significance of not forgetting one's homeland and draws parallels between the experiences of the Jewish diaspora during slavery and African colonization. The verses from Psalm 137 encapsulate the sentiment that transcends time and place – the need to cherish and remember one's homeland even in the face of adversity and displacement.

I. The Jewish Diaspora: Slavery and Remembering Zion

1. **By the Rivers of Babylon:** The psalmist's words capture the profound sorrow and longing of the Jewish people as they were exiled in Babylon. By the rivers of Babylon, they wept and their harps remained silent symbolises their

deep melancholy and disconnection from their beloved Zion.

2. **Demands for Songs of Joy:** The captors and tormentors demanded songs of joy from the exiled Jews. This juxtaposition reveals the painful irony of being asked to sing songs of joy while in a foreign land, far from the home they cherished.

3. **The Unbreakable Bond:** Despite their exile, the psalmist's vow to remember Jerusalem and maintain a deep connection to their homeland reflects the unbreakable bond between diaspora communities and their roots. It emphasizes that no matter the circumstances, the memory of home remains an integral part of their identity.

II. African Colonization: Diaspora Communities and Their Homelands

1. **African Diaspora:** The colonization of Africa resulted in the forced migration and displacement of countless African communities. The African diaspora faced immense challenges as they were uprooted from their ancestral lands and subjected to the harsh conditions of slavery and colonization.

2. **Preserving Cultural Identity:** Similar to the Jewish diaspora, African diaspora communities placed great importance on preserving their cultural identities and connections to their homelands. They carried with them traditions, languages, and memories of their ancestral homes.

III. The Unwavering Necessity of Remembering Home

1. **Identity and Resilience:** The act of remembering one's homeland is not merely a matter of sentimentality but a source of strength and resilience. It anchors diaspora

communities in their rich cultural heritage and provides a sense of belonging even in foreign lands.

2. **Cultural Continuity:** The continuity of cultural practices, languages, and traditions among diaspora communities ensures the survival and vitality of these invaluable aspects of their heritage. These cultural connections act as a bridge to the past and a beacon for future generations.

3. **Political and Social Impact:** The remembrance of one's homeland can also have political and social significance. It can serve as a rallying point for advocacy, unity, and efforts to address historical injustices and promote the rights of diaspora communities.

In conclusion, the verses from Psalm 137 and the experiences of both the Jewish diaspora during slavery and African colonization emphasize the unwavering necessity of not forgetting one's homeland. These historical narratives underscore the enduring connection between diaspora communities and their ancestral lands. Remembering home is an act of preservation, resilience, and identity. It ensures that the rich tapestry of culture and tradition continues to flourish even in the face of adversity. As history has shown, the memory of one's homeland is a beacon of hope and a testament to the enduring spirit of diaspora communities worldwide.

SELF PERCEPTION IN THE FACE OF ADVERSITY

The verse from Numbers 13:33, " *We saw Giants in the land. We seemed like grasshoppers in our own eyes, and we looked the same to them".* This verse provides a striking perspective on how the perception of oneself and how others perceive a community can shape the course of history. This section explores the perception dynamics experienced by both Jews in slavery and Africans during colonization, shedding light on how these perceptions influenced their respective journeys and legacies.

I. The Sons of Anak: Perceived Giants

1. **The Biblical Context:** The verse from Numbers is part of the account of the twelve Israelite spies sent to explore the Promised Land. When they returned, they reported seeing the sons of Anak, who they perceived as giants. In their perception, they felt as small as grasshoppers in comparison.

2. **Perception of Weakness:** The spies' perception of themselves as grasshoppers in the presence of giants reflected a sense of vulnerability and inadequacy. This perception was not only about physical size but also about power dynamics and their ability to overcome challenges.

II. Jews in Slavery: Perceived Inferiority

1. **Enslaved and Oppressed:** During their enslavement in Egypt, the Jewish people were subjected to harsh labour and oppression. They were perceived as a subordinate class, devoid of power and influence.

2. **Perception of Oppressors:** The Egyptians perceived the Jews as inferior, viewing them as a labour force rather than as equals. This perception fuelled the subjugation and mistreatment they endured.

3. **Resilience and Exodus:** Despite the perception of weakness and inferiority, the Jewish people maintained their cultural identity and resilience. Their journey, as described in the Bible, culminated in the Exodus, where they broke free from slavery, challenging the perceptions of their oppressors.

III. Africans during Colonization: Perceived as Inferior

1. **Colonial Perception:** Africans faced a similar perception of inferiority during colonization. European colonial powers often viewed African societies as primitive, uncivilized, and in need of European guidance and control.
2. **Impact on Colonization:** The perception of Africans as inferior justified colonial exploitation, including forced labour, land dispossession, and cultural suppression. It led to a system where the colonizers held power and Africans were subjugated.
3. **Struggle for Independence:** Despite being perceived as inferior, Africans across the continent fought for independence and self-determination. They challenged the colonial perception of weakness and proved their resilience and capacity for self-governance.

IV. Changing Perceptions and Legacies

1. **Changing Self-Perception:** Over time, both Jewish and African communities underwent transformations in their self-perception. They reclaimed their narratives and rejected the labels of weakness and inferiority.
2. **Legacy of Resilience:** The legacies of Jews in overcoming slavery and Africans in gaining independence are testaments to the power of changing perceptions. They demonstrate that one's perceived weakness does not define their potential or destiny.

In conclusion, the verse from Numbers 13:33 serves as a poignant reminder of the impact of perception on individuals and communities. In the face of adversity, both Jews in slavery and Africans during colonization were initially perceived as weak and inferior. However, their histories reveal that such perceptions can be challenged, reshaped, and ultimately overcome. These communities, once perceived as grasshoppers in the eyes of others, went on to demonstrate their resilience, strength, and capacity for self-determination. Their legacies serve as enduring symbols of the indomitable human spirit and the transformative power of changing one's perception and self-belief.

THE LONG-TERM EFFECT OF SLAVERY AND COLONIALISM

The effect of slavery cannot be and should never be underestimated in its consequences, though it is never the sole excuse for ignorance in any nation or generation.

However, recent research has shown that the trauma from experience can be passed on from generation to generation. And the trauma does greatly affect society and the generations that follow because they continue to harbour the sad and often traumatizing details of the type of injustice they experienced.

Dr. Rachel Yehuda, professor of psychiatry, recently researched epigenetics, and the intergenerational transmission of trauma. She investigated how severe society trauma incidents (such as slavery and Holocaust, etc.) and post-traumatic stress disorder (PTSD) are passed down through generations in shared family genes. Her research revealed that when people experience trauma over a pronounced period, it changes their genes in a particular and noticeable way. When those people have children, and their genes are passed down to their children, they also inherit the genes affected by trauma. PTSD causes the amygdala, the part of our brains that performs the primary roles of processing memory, emotional reactions, and even threat detection, to kick into overdrive. Yehuda found that the Holocaust survivors had a similar hormonal profile to Vietnam veterans suffering from PTSD.

Sociologist Dr. Joy DeGruy created the phrase Post Traumatic Slave Disorder to address the specific trauma suffered by descendants of enslaved Black people. He concluded that if the Holo-caust caused immense emotional, physical, and psychological effects that is intense enough to cause trauma to survivors, then the abject horrors and brutality suffered by slaves over many generations are more than likely to have a more pronounced impact on black slavery descendants worldwide.

Dr. DeGruy's definition of PTSD aligns with all the horrific circum-stances resulting from being subject to extreme anguish and distress over a long period. He discovered that such experiences encourage ignorance, lack of initiative and accountability, poverty, and low self-esteem. Generations that have a background of slavery find it difficult to appreciate their success in life or even the success of their relatives or friends of the same background and origin, which is the reason why it is easy for blacks to betray each other or look down on each other.

Creativity is also limited and life skills development is meagre because they are never connected to themselves or any vision of their own. Living becomes a matter of basic survival; money serves to buy food and clothing or beer if they get their hands on money. There is no plan for life or future because of not having any perspective, yet there is an urge to spend money to boost esteem by buying expensive brands. Independent thinking is taken as a sign of insubordination.

The best way to illustrate the impact of Post Traumatic Slave Disorder is the analogy of Fleas in the bottle.

The Story of the Fleas in a Bottle

"Fleas have one of the highest vertical leaps of any living insect based on size. A flea has a 36-inch vertical jump. So, if a flea is captured and put it in a bottle, a flea can jump 36-inch vertically to escape. Suppose the flea is put in a shorter jar (12-inch jar) and put the lid on the jar. Initially, the fleas will jump energetically to break free from their glass prison, aiming for the 36-inch, but it will hit its head on the jar bottle for every attempt. The flea will leap as high as it could, but the unyielding glass ceiling will thwart their every attempt.

As time passed, something remarkable happened. The flea began to adapt to their confined environment. It realised that jumping too high led to painful collisions with the glass above. In response, the flea started to limit the height of its jumps, staying well below the glass ceiling. It had learned to avoid discomfort and its jumps became more controlled and subdued.

So now the flea limit their jump capacity just to be high enough so it does not get knocked back down. Though it is able to achieve 36 inches vertical, the environment has conditioned them not to jump to their capability but only to where it will not be knocked down.

As time goes by, the flea give birth to generations of babies. They will see their parent jumping only as far as 12 inches to touch the lid. Guess what? Though the babies are born with a 36-inch vertical ability, they see their mommy and daddy, grandparent and great-great-grandparent jumping just barely to the roof. They duplicate that behaviour and never reach their potential.

Even when the glass ceiling is removed, the fleas do not spontaneously take advantage of their newfound freedom. They continued to jump only as high as the imaginary barrier that had once confined them. Despite the absence of any physical restriction, the fleas remained trapped by their own beliefs.

For generations to come, people will see the set of fleas that cannot jump high. They said they were born like that. No, they are not born like that. The environment conditioned them to be the way they are, and sometimes it takes time to adjust back to their full potential.

CHAPTER 12
THE JEWISH CULTURAL PRESERVATION

JEWISH HISTORY IS MARKED by periods of adversity, including persecution, exile, and discrimination. Throughout these challenges, Jewish communities have demonstrated remarkable resilience through the preservation of their culture. This section explores how Jewish cultural preservation has been achieved, focusing on the pivotal roles of language, religion, and education in maintaining Jewish identity and traditions.

THE ROLE OF LANGUAGE:

Hebrew: Hebrew is central to Jewish cultural preservation. Hebrew has been preserved through religious rituals, including synagogue services, the recitation of prayers, and the study of the Torah.

The Hebrew language, used in sacred texts such as the Torah, holds immense cultural and religious significance. Efforts to preserve and teach Hebrew continue to be vital aspects of Jewish cultural heritage. Biblical Hebrew, the language of the Hebrew Bible (Tanakh), served as the literary and religious language of ancient Israel. It is characterized by its use of a Semitic alphabet and distinctive grammatical features.

The revival of Hebrew as a spoken language in the late 19th and early 20th centuries is a remarkable chapter in its history. Visionaries like Eliezer Ben-Yehuda advocated for the use of Hebrew in daily life, education, and culture. It serves as a living language used in all aspects of modern Israeli society.

THE ROLE OF RELIGION

The preservation of Hebrew as a religious and cultural language has played a vital role in maintaining Jewish identity. It serves as a unifying linguistic thread among Jewish communities regardless of their geographical location. The observance of Jewish holidays, dietary laws, and the Sabbath reinforces the bonds of Jewish communities.

Synagogue and Prayer: Synagogues have served as centres for communal worship, study, and cultural exchange, fostering a sense of belonging and continuity. The regular recitation of prayers in Hebrew reinforces Jewish linguistic and religious traditions.

Community centres, Jewish cultural festivals, and events provide opportunities for Jews to come together, share their heritage, and pass it on to the younger generation. Jewish children receive religious education through formal settings, such as Hebrew schools, and informal education within families and communities. The study of Torah, Talmud, and Jewish history instils a deep understanding of Jewish culture, ethics, and identity.

THE ROLE OF EDUCATION:

Jewish Schools and Institutions: Jewish communities have established educational institutions to ensure the transmission of cultural and religious knowledge to future generations. Yeshivas, Jewish day schools, and educational organizations play pivotal roles in educating Jewish youth.

Holocaust Education: The Holocaust, while a painful chapter in Jewish history, is taught as a means of preserving memory and instilling a commitment to combating hatred and intolerance. Holocaust museums and educational programs worldwide aim to ensure that future generations never forget the atrocities of the past.

JEWISH CULTURAL EXPRESSIONS

Art and Music: Jewish art and music have played a crucial role in cultural preservation. Artists like Marc Chagall and musicians like Leonard Bernstein have contributed to the rich tapestry of Jewish cultural expression. Klezmer music, rooted in Eastern European Jewish culture, continues to be celebrated worldwide for its lively and expressive melodies.

Literature and Storytelling: Jewish literature has produced a wealth of influential works, from the biblical texts to modern Jewish literature by authors like Isaac Bashevis Singer and Philip Roth.

Food and Cuisine: Jewish cuisine reflects the diversity of Jewish culture with distinct dishes and culinary traditions from Ashkenazi, Sephardic, Mizrahi, and other Jewish communities. Jewish food, including bagels, matzo ball soup, and challah, has become an integral part of global cuisine, preserving cultural flavours and traditions.

Commemoration and Memory: Jewish communities worldwide engage in commemorative practices, such as Holocaust memorials, Yom HaShoah (Holocaust Remembrance Day), and Tisha B'Av (a day of mourning).

Jewish cultural preservation not only ensures the continuity of a rich and diverse tradition but also fosters a deep sense of identity and connection among Jewish communities worldwide. It serves as a source of inspiration and a testament to the enduring strength of a people who have persevered through history while contributing significantly to the global cultural tapestry.

THE JEWISH CONNECTION TO ISRAEL

Israel as a Cultural Anchor: The establishment of the State of Israel in 1948 has had a profound impact on Jewish cultural preservation. Israel serves as a cultural anchor as it offers a physical homeland where Jewish traditions, language, and religious practices are upheld and celebrated.

Pilgrimage and Connection: Israel remains a destination of pilgrimage for Jews worldwide, reinforcing a sense of connection to their historical and religious roots.

Visitors to Israel experience firsthand the continuity of Jewish culture, from ancient archaeological sites to contemporary cultural expressions.

CHALLENGES AND CONTEMPORARY DYNAMICS

Assimilation and Intermarriage: In modern times, Jewish communities face the challenge of assimilation and intermarriage, which can lead to a dilution of cultural traditions. Efforts to address these challenges often involve initiatives to engage young Jews in cultural and religious education.

Adaptation to Modernity: The Jewish community has embraced technological and social changes while adapting traditional practices to contemporary life.

The digital age has provided new avenues for cultural preservation with online resources, virtual synagogue services, and educational platforms.

CHAPTER 13
THE AFRICAN RESILIENCE AMIDST SLAVERY'S BRUTALITY

THE AFRICAN EXPERIENCE during the transatlantic slave trade is a testament to the indomitable spirit of a people who, despite enduring unimaginable brutality and displacement, managed to preserve their cultural elements. This section explores how African cultural elements survived the horrors of slavery as they were transmitted through oral traditions, music, and religious practices, leaving an enduring legacy.

THE RESILIENCE AND SURVIVAL OF AFRICAN TRIBE DURING SLAVERY

The history of the African Diaspora in North America is marked by unimaginable suffering and resilience. Enslaved Africans brought with them a rich tapestry of cultures, languages, and traditions from the African continent and thus contributed to the diverse cultural mosaic of the Americas. Among the numerous African ethnic groups, we will focus on the Yoruba people. The Yoruba people, who hail from what is now Nigeria and Benin, played a significant role in shaping the cultural, spiritual, and intellectual heritage of African Americans. This section explores how this tribe survived and left a legacy during the era of slavery in North America.

The Yoruba people are one of the largest and most culturally rich ethnic groups in West Africa. They are renowned for their complex religious and spiritual traditions, artistry, music, and strong sense of community. As a result of the transatlantic slave trade, many Yoruba individuals were forcibly transported to North America where they faced unimaginable challenges to their identity and culture.

II. Cultural Resilience

Retention of Yoruba Language and Traditions: One of the remarkable aspects of the Yoruba survival is the preservation of their language and cultural practices. Despite the forced separation from their homeland, Yoruba captives managed to keep their language alive by incorporating Yoruba words, phrases, and idioms into Creole languages and dialects spoken on plantations. Elements of Yoruba culture, such as storytelling, proverbs, and folklore, were also passed down through generations.

Religious Adaptation: The Yoruba religion, often referred to as Yoruba spirituality or Orisha worship, remained a vital part of Yoruba identity even in the face of slavery. Enslaved Yoruba people adapted their religious practices to the new environment, often blending Yoruba beliefs with elements of Christianity, and created syncretic religions like Santeria in Cuba and Candomblé in Brazil.

Resilience and Spiritual Continuity: African Diaspora religions provided enslaved Africans with a means to maintain their spiritual continuity. Despite the harsh conditions of slavery, these religions allowed them to connect with their ancestral traditions, gods, and spiritual practices.

Resistance and Identity: These religions became vehicles of resistance against the dehumanizing aspects of slavery. Enslaved individuals used rituals and ceremonies to assert their autonomy, foster a sense of community, and resist oppression. For example, the Haitian Revolution was significantly influenced by Vodou practices.

Community and Social Cohesion: African Diaspora religions fostered a sense of community and social cohesion among enslaved individuals. They provided spaces for communal gatherings, mutual support, and the sharing of cultural knowledge.

Preservation of Cosmology: African religious cosmologies, which emphasized ancestral veneration and the importance of nature, persisted in diaspora communities. Elements of African belief systems can still be observed in various Afro-Caribbean, Afro-Brazilian, and Afro-Latinx religious practices.

Resistance and Uprisings: The Yoruba people participated in various forms of resistance against slavery, including organized revolts. The most famous of these revolts was the 1811 German Coast Uprising in Louisiana where Yoruba and other enslaved Africans fought for their freedom.

THE SIGNIFICANCE OF TRIBAL MARKS DURING AFRICAN SLAVERY

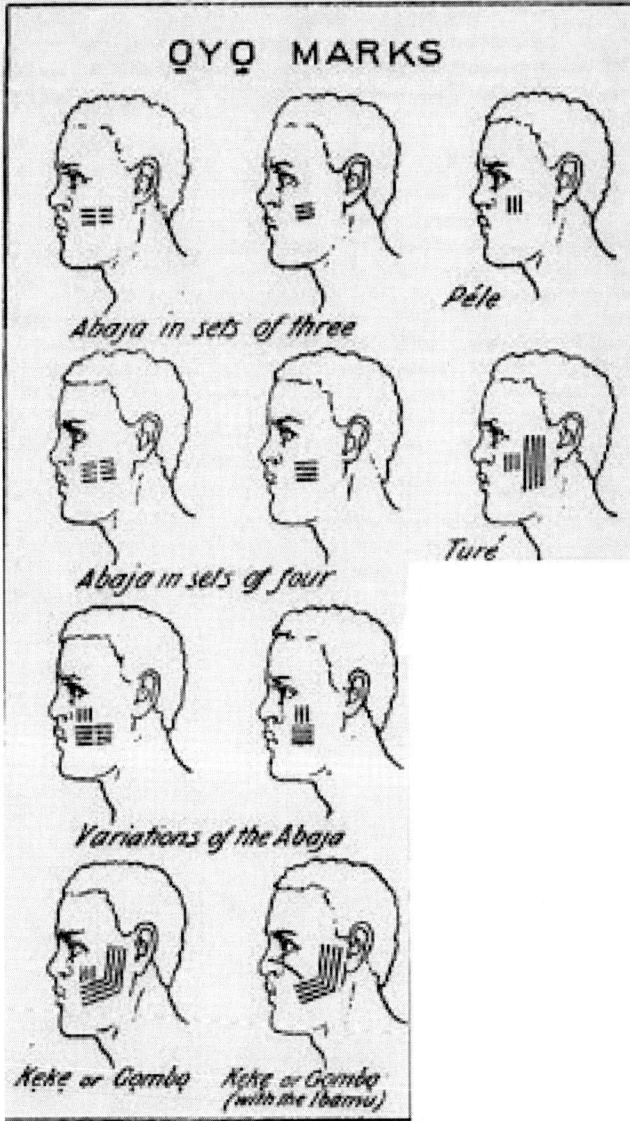

ỌYỌ MARKS

Abaja in sets of three

Pélé

Abaja in sets of four

Turé

Variations of the Abaja

Kẹkẹ or Gọmbọ   Kẹkẹ or Gọmbọ
(with the Ibamu)

Cultural Identity: Tribal marks served as visual markers of cultural identity. They were a form of body modification that denoted a person's ethnic or tribal affiliation. These marks varied widely in design, location, and meaning and reflected the rich diversity of African cultures.

Resilience and Connection to Ancestry: Despite the traumatic experiences of slavery, many Africans held onto their cultural practices, including tribal marks. These marks served as a link to their ancestral heritage, providing a sense of continuity and identity in the face of adversity.

Communication and Significance: Tribal marks were not arbitrary; they conveyed information about an individual's lineage, social status, or life experiences. Different patterns and locations of marks held specific meanings within each culture. They could indicate one's age, marital status, or clan membership.

Identity Amidst Dehumanization: Enslaved Africans were subjected to dehumanizing conditions, including forced labour and the stripping of their names and identities. Tribal marks, however, allowed them to maintain a sense of self and belonging within a hostile environment.

Psychological Comfort: Tribal marks provided psychological comfort and a sense of community. During the isolation and cruelty of slavery, they served as a reminder of one's roots and a connection to a larger cultural framework.

Tribal marks during African slavery were more than just physical inscriptions on the skin; they were symbols of cultural identity, resilience, and resistance. In a context where the humanity and identities of enslaved Africans were systematically stripped away, tribal marks provided a means of preserving cultural heritage and maintaining a connection to one's roots. The significance of these marks extends beyond the physical; they are a testament to the enduring strength of African cultures and the indomitable spirit of those who endured the horrors of slavery.

MUSIC AND DANCE

Jazz: Emerging in the United States in the late 19th and early 20th centuries, jazz music is deeply rooted in African rhythms and improvisational techniques. It has since become a global phenomenon, influencing numerous music genres.

Blues: The blues, with its origins in African American communities, has played a pivotal role in shaping rock, pop, and contemporary music.

Hip-Hop: Hip-hop, born in African American and Afro-Latino communities in New York City, has become a global cultural and musical movement, influencing fashion, language, and visual arts.

Literature: African American Literature: Writers like Langston Hughes, Zora Neale Hurston, and James Baldwin have made significant contributions to American and world literature, addressing themes of race, identity, and social justice.

Caribbean Literature: Authors like Jamaica Kincaid, Derek Walcott, and Edwidge Danticat have received international acclaim, exploring the complexities of Caribbean identity and colonial history.

Contemporary Artists: Contemporary African and African diaspora artists like Kehinde Wiley, Yinka Shonibare, and Kara Walker have gained global recognition for their thought-provoking works.

CUISINE:

The culinary heritage of Black Africa is a testament to the resilience, resourcefulness, and cultural richness of the African people. This culinary journey, often overlooked, has a profound legacy that extends across the Atlantic Ocean, influencing the foodways, flavours, and traditions of the African diaspora in the Americas.

African cuisine is as diverse as the continent itself, with each region boasting its unique ingredients, techniques, and dishes. From the fiery stews of West Africa to the aromatic biryanis of East Africa, the culinary tapestry is woven with ingredients like yams, okra, plantains, millet, and spices such as cayenne, cardamom, and coriander.

One remarkable aspect of African cuisine is its strong connection to the land. Many traditional dishes are based on locally sourced ingredients, emphasizing the importance of sustainability and harmony with nature. Moreover, communal cooking and shared meals are integral to African culture, fostering a sense of togetherness and unity within communities.

In the Americas, enslaved Africans played a central role in shaping the emerging food culture. They drew upon their knowledge of African ingredients and cooking techniques to create new dishes using locally available resources. The fusion of African, Indigenous, and European culinary traditions gave birth to what we now recognize as African diaspora cuisine.

One of the most enduring legacies of Black African cuisine in the Americas is soul food. Soul food is a celebration of African culinary heritage characterized by dishes like collard greens, black-eyed peas, fried chicken, cornbread, and gumbo.

African cuisine is a testament to resourcefulness as it often relies on humble ingredients that are readily available. Staples like cassava, yams, plantains, millet, and legumes serve as the foundation of many African dishes. These ingredients are not only affordable but also highly nutritious, providing sustenance to communities across the continent.

Soul food also places a strong emphasis on communal dining and echoes the African tradition of shared meals. It became a symbol of resilience, a way for African Americans to maintain a connection to their cultural roots despite the horrors of slavery and segregation.

Caribbean Cuisine: Caribbean cuisine, influenced by African, Indigenous, and European flavours, has gained popularity world-wide with dishes like jerk chicken and plantains.

In today's globalized world, African flavours and cooking techniques are making their mark on international culinary scenes. From the ubiquity of spicy peri-peri sauces to the growing popularity of dishes like jollof rice and injera, African cuisine is gaining recognition and appreciation worldwide.

The culinary journey and legacy of Black Africa across the Atlantic are a testament to the enduring power of culture and cuisine.

INFLUENCE OF BLACK PEOPLE ON SPORT

The influence of Black people on sports is profound, far-reaching, and continues to shape the world of athletics in various ways. From breaking barriers and challenging racial stereotypes to inspiring social change and introducing innovative styles of play, Black athletes have left an indelible mark on the sporting landscape.

Breaking Barriers and Challenging Stereotypes - Black athletes have been instrumental in breaking racial barriers and challenging deeply entrenched stereotypes in sports. Icons like Jackie Robinson, who became the first African American to play Major League Baseball in 1947, paved the way for future generations of Black athletes to compete at the highest levels of professional sports.

Excellence in a Multitude of Sports - Black athletes have excelled in a multitude of sports, showcasing their versatility and athleticism. From track and field, where athletes like Usain Bolt have set world records, to basketball, where legends like Michael Jordan and LeBron James have dominated, Black athletes have consistently demonstrated their prowess in various disciplines.

Social Activism and Advocacy - Many Black athletes have used their platforms to advocate for social justice and raise awareness of important issues. Figures like Colin Kaepernick, who knelt during the national anthem to protest racial injustice, have ignited important conversations about race and inequality. Their activism highlights the intersection of sports and social change and shows that athletes can be powerful advocates for justice.

CONTEMPORARY INFLUENCE OF BLACK AFRICANS ON SCIENCE AND INNOVATION

The narrative of scientific and innovative contributions has long been dominated by Western voices, but as the global landscape evolves, so too does the face of scientific discovery. In recent years, there has been a significant and growing influence of Black Africans on the world of science and innovation. This influence extends across various fields, from technology and medicine to space exploration and environmental sustainability, challenging stereotypes and reshaping our understanding of global contributions to human progress.

Medicine and Healthcare Advancements: Black Africans have made substantial strides in the field of medicine. Dr. Clet Niyikiza, a Burundian-born scientist, played a pivotal role in the development of anti-cancer drugs. Dr. Tshilidzi Marwala, a South African engineer, combines artificial intelligence and healthcare to improve patient outcomes.

African scientists and healthcare workers have been at the forefront of research and response during global health crises, such as the Ebola and COVID 19 outbreaks, showcasing their expertise in epidemic control and management.

Technology and Innovation: The tech sector in Africa is experiencing rapid growth. Innovators like Iyinoluwa Aboyeji from Nigeria co-founded Andela and Flutterwave, two companies driving tech solutions for global markets. African entrepreneurs are creating e-commerce platforms, fintech solutions, and mobile apps that address local and international needs, demonstrating the continent's tech prowess. Philip Emeagwali is the highly gifted Super Computer genius.

Space Exploration and Research: Dr. Maggie Aderin-Pocock, a British-Nigerian space scientist, has popularized space science in the UK and globally and inspires a new generation of scientists.

African countries like Nigeria and South Africa are investing in space research and satellite technology, contributing to global efforts in telecommunications, weather forecasting, and disaster management.

Programs like "Hidden Figures No More" recognize the historical and contemporary achievements of Black women in space exploration.

Representation and Advocacy: African scientists are breaking barriers in academia, research institutions, and international organizations, advocating for more equitable representation and recognition in global scientific forums.

In conclusion, the contemporary influence of Black Africans on science and innovation is undeniably transformative. These scientists, researchers, and innovators are not only driving progress within their communities but also shaping the global landscape of discovery and innovation. As their contributions continue to gain recognition, the world is becoming increasingly aware of the wealth of talent and expertise that Black Africans bring to the forefront of science and innovation, inspiring positive change and fostering a more inclusive future for all.

CHAPTER 14
THE JEWISH STRUGGLE FOR IDENTITY

THE JEWISH STRUGGLE FOR IDENTITY, emancipation, and the establishment of the State of Israel is a complex and multifaceted narrative that spans centuries. This section delves into the evolving Jewish identity, the quest for emancipation from discrimination and persecution, and the eventual realization of a Jewish homeland in the form of the State of Israel.

A Perennial Diaspora: Shaping Jewish Identity

The Enlightenment Era: The Enlightenment of the 18th century introduced the ideals of reason, individualism, and equality in Europe. The Enlightenment was characterized by a profound shift in thinking. It emphasized the primacy of reason and individualism, championing the idea that humans possessed the capacity for rational thought and could use it to improve their lives and society. Enlightenment thinkers sought to challenge the dogma and superstitions of the past and advocated for intellectual freedom and the pursuit of knowledge through empirical observation and critical thinking.

The Enlightenment had far-reaching effects on politics, science, philosophy, and society. Enlightenment ideas inspired political revolutions, including the American Revolution (1775-1783) and the French Revolution (1789-1799), which ushered in an era of constitutionalism and secular governance. Enlightenment ideals of liberty, equality, and justice contributed to the development of human rights principles and modern democracy. The separation of church and state became a foundational principle in many democratic societies, promoting religious freedom and tolerance.

These ideas sparked a desire for emancipation among European Jews, who sought equal rights and integration into secular society.

Struggles for Emancipation: The Jewish struggle for emancipation, particularly in Europe, spanned centuries and was characterized by a relentless quest for equality, civil rights, and full citizenship. This struggle unfolded against a backdrop of prejudice, discrimination, and political upheaval.

Before the era of emancipation, Jews in Europe often lived in segregated communities, subject to restrictive laws and discriminatory practices. They were often confined to specific professions, denied land ownership, and excluded from political participation. One significant event in this period was the Spanish Inquisition (1478-1834), which expelled or forcibly converted many Sephardic Jews. The Naturalization Act of 1753 had prohibited Jews from becoming naturalized British citizens.

The Enlightenment, with its emphasis on reason, individualism, and secularism, played a pivotal role in shaping the Jewish struggle for emancipation. Enlightenment thinkers challenged traditional notions of hierarchy and advocated for the rights of individuals, including religious minorities. Key Enlightenment philosophers like Voltaire and John Locke expressed support for Jewish emancipation.

Zionist Movement: The Quest for a Homeland

The late 19th century witnessed the emergence of the Zionist movement, led by Theodor Herzl and others. Zionism aimed to establish a Jewish homeland, recognizing that the persistent diaspora left Jews vulnerable to discrimination and persecution.

The Balfour Declaration and Mandate Period: During World War I, the Balfour Declaration (1917) expressed British support for a "national home for the Jewish people" in Palestine. The subsequent British Mandate over Palestine (1920-1948) marked a pivotal period in the Zionist quest for statehood.

The Holocaust and Post-War Immigration: The Holocaust (1941-1945) resulted in the systematic murder of six million Jews by Nazi Germany. The horrors of the Holocaust underscored the urgent need for a Jewish homeland and contributed to international support for Jewish migration to Palestine.

THE JEWISH HOLOCAUST

The Holocaust, one of the most horrifying and genocidal events in human history, unfolded during World War II under the regime of Adolf Hitler's Nazi Germany. Its primary target was the Jewish population of Europe. The Holocaust occurred against the backdrop of World War II, a global conflict that ravaged Europe and beyond. Adolf Hitler, who came to power in Germany in 1933, propagated virulent anti-Semitic ideologies.

The Nuremberg Laws of 1935 stripped Jews of their citizenship, rights, and protections and paved the way for escalating persecution.

Systematic Nature of the Holocaust: The Holocaust was not a random act of violence but a meticulously planned and executed genocide. The "Final Solution," conceived during the Wannsee Conference in 1942, aimed at the systematic extermination of Europe's Jewish population.

Concentration camps, extermination camps (such as Auschwitz and Sobibor), and mass shootings were among the methods used to annihilate millions of Jews.

Human Toll: Approximately six million Jews, including men, women, and children, perished in the Holocaust. They were subjected to forced labour, starvation, medical experiments, and mass killings in gas chambers. Jewish communities across Europe were decimated and countless families were torn apart.

Resistance and Resilience: Despite overwhelming odds, Jewish resistance movements, such as the Warsaw Ghetto Uprising, demonstrated acts of bravery and defiance.

Liberation and Nuremberg Trials: Allied forces liberated concentration camps as they advanced through Europe. The shocking scenes they encountered spurred international outrage.

The Nuremberg Trials held Nazi leaders accountable for war crimes and crimes against humanity, setting a precedent for international justice.

DP Camps: DP camps were administered by Allied forces, primarily in Germany, Austria, and Italy. They housed Holocaust survivors, former forced laborers, and refugees from Eastern Europe.

These camps served as temporary homes for survivors, providing them with medical treatment, education, and vocational training.

Immigration and Resettlement: Survivors sought opportunities to rebuild their lives. For many, this meant emigrating to countries where they could start anew. The founding of the State of Israel in 1948 had a profound impact on Jewish survivors as it provided a homeland where they could begin anew.

Other countries, including the United States, Canada, Australia, and various European nations, also welcomed Jewish survivors and offered them refuge.

Legal and Financial Compensation: After the war, efforts were made to hold Nazi officials accountable for their crimes. The Nuremberg Trials and subsequent legal actions sought justice for Holocaust victims.

The Conference on Jewish Material Claims Against Germany (Claims Conference) played a significant role in negotiating reparations and restitution agreements for Holocaust survivors and their heirs.

Commemoration and Memory: Holocaust survivors and their descendants have been instrumental in preserving the memory of the Holocaust through museums, memorials, and educational initiatives.

Holocaust remembrance serves as a reminder of the importance of preventing genocide and fostering tolerance and human rights.

Ongoing Challenges: Many survivors and their families faced lifelong challenges related to physical and emotional scars from the Holocaust. The memory of the Holocaust continues to shape discussions about genocide prevention, Holocaust education, and the responsibility to remember. The Holocaust and its aftermath remain an indelible part of human history, serving as a stark reminder of the consequences of hatred and intolerance. The resilience and determination of survivors in rebuilding their lives and ensuring that the world remembers this dark period stand as a testament to the strength of the human spirit.

Lessons and Legacy: The Holocaust stands as a stark reminder of the consequences of unchecked hatred, prejudice, and intolerance. It underscores the importance of promoting human rights, dignity, and diversity.

In conclusion, the Jewish Holocaust remains an indelible stain on human history, a testament to the depths of cruelty humanity can sink to. Its memory obliges us to confront intolerance, hatred, and prejudice in all forms. By remembering the Holocaust, we honour the memory of its victims and survivors and reaffirm our commitment to a world where the darkest chapters of history are not repeated. It is a solemn vow to ensure that the six million lives lost are never forgotten and the lessons of the Holocaust continue to guide our pursuit of a more just and humane world.

A COMPARATIVE ANALYSIS OF THE HOLOCAUST AND THE CONGOLESE GENOCIDE

The Holocaust and the Congolese Genocide are two of the darkest chapters in human history, marked by mass atrocities, suffering, and immense loss of life. While these events occurred in different contexts and eras, they share several striking similarities and differences and offer important lessons about the consequences of hatred, prejudice, and unchecked power.

Congolese Genocide (1885-1908):

The Congolese Genocide occurred during the colonization of the Congo by King Leopold II of Belgium. It was a result of ruthless exploitation and abuse of the Congolese population for rubber and ivory production. While it was not characterized by mass extermination camps like the Holocaust, it led to the deaths of an estimated 10 million Congolese due to violence, forced labor, and disease.

Similarities:

1. Dehumanization: Both the Holocaust and the Congolese Genocide involved the dehumanization of targeted groups. In the Holocaust, Jews were subjected to racist propaganda and stereotypes while the Congolese were treated as subhuman by European colonizers.

2. Economic Exploitation: Economic interests played a significant role in both genocides. The Holocaust saw the plundering of

Jewish property and assets while the Congolese Genocide aimed at extracting rubber and ivory for profit.

3. Brutality and Violence: Both events were characterized by extreme brutality and violence. The Holocaust had extermination camps like Auschwitz while the Congolese Genocide witnessed massacres, mutilation, and widespread violence.

4. International Apathy: Both genocides occurred in the context of international apathy or ignorance. The world was slow to respond to the Holocaust just as the atrocities in the Congo were often downplayed or ignored by European powers.

Legacy and Lessons: Both the Holocaust and the Congolese Genocide serve as somber reminders of the consequences of unchecked hatred, prejudice, and exploitation. They underline the importance of recognizing and confronting such atrocities promptly. These events have led to efforts to prevent genocide, promote human rights, and ensure accountability for war crimes and crimes against humanity.

Legacy of Accountability: The Holocaust and the Congolese Genocide have left a lasting legacy of accountability. The Nuremberg Trials held after World War II established a precedent for prosecuting individuals responsible for war crimes and crimes against humanity. Similarly, international efforts have called for accountability for crimes committed during the Congolese Genocide, although challenges in achieving justice persist.

Impact on Collective Memory: Both genocides have had a profound impact on the collective memory. Holocaust remembrance, education, and museums like Yad Vashem in Israel ensure that the memory of the Holocaust endures with a commitment to "never forget." In the case of the Congolese Genocide, efforts are underway to remember and acknowledge the suffering of the Congolese people, although much work remains to fully recognize and memorialize these events.

Influence on Human Rights Movements: The Holocaust played a pivotal role in shaping the modern human rights movement. The horrors of the Holocaust contributed to the development of international human rights instruments and organizations, such as the Universal Declaration of Human Rights and the United Nations. Similarly, the Congolese Genocide has prompted discussions on colonial-era injustices and their impact on contemporary human rights advocacy.

Global Awareness and Prevention: Both genocides have contributed to global awareness of the consequences of unchecked hatred and violence. They have reinforced the importance of early intervention and prevention of mass atrocities. International organizations, NGOs, and activists draw on the lessons of these genocides to advocate for peace, conflict resolution, and the protection of vulnerable populations.

Challenges in Acknowledgment and Reconciliation: Acknowledging the atrocities of the Holocaust and the Congolese Genocide and achieving reconciliation remain ongoing challenges. While there have been significant efforts to commemorate the Holocaust and educate future generations, addressing the historical injustices of the Congolese Genocide and its impact on contemporary Congolese society requires continued attention and reconciliation efforts.

In conclusion, the Holocaust and the Congolese Genocide, despite their differences in scale, motivation, and context, share a common legacy of suffering, injustice, and the need for remembrance. They serve as stark reminders of humanity's capacity for cruelty and the importance of vigilance in preventing genocide and mass atrocities. By studying and remembering these events, we honor the victims, work towards accountability and justice, and commit ourselves to a future where such horrors are never repeated.

A COMPARATIVE ANALYSIS OF THE HOLOCAUST AND THE HERERO AND NAMAQUA GENOCIDE

The Holocaust and the Herero and Namaqua Genocide are two dark chapters in human history marked by mass atrocities, suffering, and immense loss of life. While these events occurred in different contexts and eras, they share significant similarities and differences and provide important insights into the consequences of hatred, colonialism, and unchecked power.

Herero and Namaqua Genocide (1904-1908): The Herero and Namaqua Genocide occurred during German colonial rule in what is now Namibia. German forces, led by General Lothar von Trotha, sought to suppress a rebellion by the Herero and Nama peoples. This brutal campaign led to the deaths of an estimated 75,000 Herero and Nama individuals, largely through violence, forced labor, and deprivation.

Similarities:

1. **Dehumanization:** Both the Holocaust and the Herero and Namaqua Genocide involved the dehumanization of targeted groups. The Nazis propagated anti-Semitic propaganda and portrayed Jews as subhuman while German colonial authorities dehumanized the Herero and Nama as "savages."
2. **Systematic Violence:** Both events were characterized by systematic violence. The Holocaust had extermination camps like Auschwitz, Sobibor, and Treblinka while the Herero and Namaqua Genocide saw massacres, forced marches, and concentration camps.
3. **Economic Interests:** Economic interests played a significant role in both genocides. In the Holocaust, Jews were subjected to slave labor, and their assets were plundered. In the Herero and Namaqua Genocide,

German colonial authorities aimed to seize land and resources.

4. **International Apathy:** Both genocides occurred in the context of international apathy or ignorance. The world was slow to respond to the Holocaust, just as the atrocities in German South-West Africa (now Namibia) were downplayed or overlooked by European powers.

Both the Holocaust and the Herero and Namaqua Genocide underscore the consequences of unchecked hatred, colonialism, and exploitation. They emphasize the importance of acknowledging historical injustices and working towards reconciliation, justice, and the prevention of future genocides.

In conclusion, while the Holocaust and the Herero and Namaqua Genocide unfolded in different times and contexts, their shared characteristics of dehumanization, systematic violence, economic interests, and international apathy highlight the need for vigilance in preventing and addressing genocide and mass atrocities. Studying these events not only honors the memory of the victims but also reminds us of our collective responsibility to prevent such horrors from happening in the future.

A COMPARATIVE ANALYSIS OF NAZI AND BRITISH CONCENTRATION CAMPS IN KENYA

Nazi concentration camps during World War II and British concentration camps during the Mau Mau uprising in Kenya are two historical instances marked by mass internment, suffering, and grave human rights violations. While these events occurred in different contexts and eras, they share significant similarities and differences, offering insights into the consequences of colonialism, conflict, and the treatment of detainees.

British Concentration Camps in Kenya (1950s): During the Mau Mau uprising against British colonial rule in Kenya, the British established concentration camps to detain suspected Mau Mau insurgents. These camps were used to suppress the rebellion and resulted in the internment of thousands of Kenyan detainees, including women and children. The treatment of detainees in these camps led to allegations of widespread human rights abuses.

Similarities:

1. **Mass Internment:** Both Nazi concentration camps and British concentration camps in Kenya involved the mass internment of individuals. Nazi camps detained millions of people while British camps in Kenya held thousands.
2. **Human Rights Abuses:** Both sets of camps were marked by severe human rights abuses. Nazi concentration camps saw the systematic extermination of millions through mass killings, forced labor, and medical experiments. British concentration camps in Kenya witnessed allegations of torture, abuse, and deprivation of detainees' rights.
3. **Dehumanization:** Both systems involved the dehumanization of detainees. Nazi propaganda portrayed Jews and other targeted groups as subhuman while British authorities dehumanized Mau Mau suspects as "rebels" and "terrorists."
4. **International Reaction:** The existence of both sets of camps initially faced international indifference or ignorance. The world was slow to respond to the horrors of Nazi concentration camps, just as the British concentration camps in Kenya operated with limited international scrutiny.

The legacy of Nazi concentration camps is synonymous with the Holocaust and has significantly shaped discussions on human rights, genocide prevention, and the responsibility to protect. The British concentration camps in Kenya are associated with the broader history of colonialism and decolonization in Africa.

In conclusion. while Nazi concentration camps and British concentration camps in Kenya were distinct in terms of motivation, scale, and historical context, they both represent grave human rights violations and highlight the need for accountability, justice, and the prevention of future abuses.

REPARATIONS FOR THE HOLOCAUST SURVIVORS

In recognition of this unprecedented tragedy, the issue of reparations for Holocaust survivors and their descendants has been a matter of intense debate, legal action, and moral consideration. This section explores the moral imperative behind reparations for Holocaust survivors.

The Scale of the Holocaust: The Holocaust was an unparalleled catastrophe that left deep scars on the Jewish people and humanity as a whole. The sheer scale of the atrocity, with millions of innocent lives brutally extinguished, underscores the enormity of the moral debt owed to survivors.

The Trauma of Survivors: Holocaust survivors endured physical, psychological, and emotional trauma that continued long after the war ended. Many faced the loss of family members, homes, possessions, and their sense of security. Survivors often struggled with survivor's guilt, post-traumatic stress disorder (PTSD), and other mental health issues.

The Loss of Livelihood: In addition to personal losses, Holocaust survivors often lost their livelihoods, properties, and assets due to persecution and confiscation by the Nazi regime. After the war, they faced the immense challenge of rebuilding their lives from scratch.

The Responsibility of Perpetrators: Germany, as the perpetrator of the Holocaust, bore a significant moral responsibility to provide reparations to survivors. Recognizing this responsibility, Germany, under Chancellor Konrad Adenauer, initiated reparation payments to Holocaust survivors and the State of Israel in the early 1950s. This marked a significant step in acknowledging the moral debt owed to survivors.

The Legal Framework: International law, including the Genocide Convention, recognizes the obligation of states to provide reparations to victims of genocide. Holocaust survivors and their families were the victims of a genocidal regime and this legal framework supports the moral argument for reparations.

Reparations as a Moral Imperative: Reparations for Holocaust survivors are not merely a matter of financial compensation; they represent a moral imperative for several reasons:

1. **Acknowledgment of Responsibility:** Reparations signify a recognition of the moral responsibility borne by the perpetrators and their descendants. They acknowledge the horrors of the past and the enduring suffering of survivors.
2. **Symbolic Justice:** Reparations symbolize a form of justice and a commitment to addressing historical wrongs. They send a powerful message that the world will not forget or condone such atrocities.
3. **Support for Survivors:** Many Holocaust survivors and their descendants faced significant challenges in rebuilding their lives. Reparations provide much-needed support for aging survivors and help address the economic hardships they endured.
4. **Moral Obligation:** Providing reparations is a way for the international community to fulfill its moral obligation to the survivors and their families. It reflects the core principles of human rights and dignity.

In conclusion, reparations for Holocaust survivors are a moral imperative rooted in the recognition of historical atrocities, the responsibility of perpetrators, and the international legal framework. While reparations cannot fully heal the wounds of the past, they represent a meaningful step toward acknowledging the suffering endured by survivors and their families. They serve as a testament to the commitment of society to ensure that such horrors are never repeated and that the memory of the Holocaust endures as a reminder of the moral duty to protect human rights and dignity.

Germany signed its first Holocaust reparations, the Luxembourg Agreement, with Israel in 1952 and has since then agreed to around 80 billion euros in payments negotiated with the claims conference, which has also pushed to expand the scope of compensation from those interned in concentration camps to those who survived ghettos as well as to those who were small children during Nazi occupation.

Other payments include, 12 million euros ($11.96 million) of emergency humanitarian payments was given to 8,500 Ukrainian Holocaust survivors and 170 million euros ($166 million) will go to a special hardship fund that will impact approximately 143,000 Holocaust survivors worldwide.

As the number of Holocaust survivors dwindles, teaching the coming generations about the atrocities committed during the genocide of the Jewish people becomes ever more important. Therefore, Germany agreed for the first time in the negotiations to specifically fund Holocaust education — with 10 million euros for 2022, 25 million euros for 2023, 30 million euros for 2024 and 35 million euros for 2025.

THE INJUSTICE OF THE LACK OF REPARATIONS FOR TRANSATLANTIC SLAVERY

The transatlantic slave trade, one of history's most brutal and dehumanizing episodes, led to the enslavement of millions of Africans over centuries. The echoes of this profound injustice continue to reverberate in the form of systemic racism, socio-economic disparities, and ongoing racial discrimination. This section delves into the profound injustice of the lack of reparations for transatlantic slavery and the moral imperative for addressing this historical wrong.

1. The Legacy of Enslavement: The enslavement of Africans in the Americas resulted in the forced labor, brutal treatment, and dehumanization of millions. This legacy of exploitation and oppression has had enduring consequences for descendants of enslaved Africans, including economic, social, and psychological impacts.

2. Reparations as a Moral Imperative: Reparations for transatlantic slavery represent a moral imperative rooted in principles of justice, human rights, and historical responsibility.

The moral argument is grounded in the acknowledgment of historical wrongs and the responsibility of the beneficiaries of slavery to address the ongoing impact of that injustice.

3. Economic Exploitation: Enslaved Africans were subjected to extreme economic exploitation. Their forced labor generated immense wealth for European colonizers and laid the economic foundations of modern Western nations.

4. Social and Economic Disparities: The lack of reparations has perpetuated social and economic disparities that disproportionately affect Black communities in the Americas and Europe. These disparities manifest in areas such as income, education, housing, and healthcare.

5. Ongoing Racial Discrimination: Racial discrimination and systemic racism persist as deeply entrenched issues in societies that participated in the transatlantic slave trade. The lack of reparations contributes to the perpetuation of racial injustices.

6. International Precedents: Reparations for historical injustices have been granted in other contexts. For example, reparations were provided to Japanese-Americans who were interned during World War II and to Holocaust survivors.

7. Movements for Reparations: There have been ongoing movements and advocacy for reparations for transatlantic slavery, including calls for acknowledgment, apologies, and compensation.

8. Truth and Reconciliation: Reparations are often seen as a critical component of truth and reconciliation processes as they allow societies to confront their past and work toward healing and justice.

9. Addressing Historical Responsibility: Reparations serve as a means for modern societies to take responsibility for their historical actions and the enduring consequences of those actions.

Calculating the exact worth of reparations for Black Africa slavery involves analysing various facts and figures, but it's important to note that precise calculations are highly complex and subject to debate. Nonetheless, here are some key factors and data points that can be considered:

1. **Enslaved Individuals:** An estimated 12.5 million Africans were forcibly transported to the Americas during the transatlantic slave trade. This number serves as a starting point for assessing the scale of the injustice. By the mid-19th century, a skilled, able-bodied enslaved person could fetch up to $2,000, although prices varied by the state.
2. **Labor Exploitation:** Enslaved Africans provided unpaid labour that contributed significantly to the economic development of the Americas, particularly in agriculture, mining, and other industries. The monetary value of this labour, adjusted for historical economic conditions, can be considered.
3. **Economic Gains in the Americas:** The wealth generated from enslaved labour had profound and enduring effects on the economies of the Americas and Europe. Estimates

of the economic benefits that accrued to slave-owning societies could be part of reparations calculations.

4. **Impact on Africa:** Reparations should also address the economic and social consequences of depopulation, disrupted societies, and lost opportunities for economic development in Africa.

5. **Property and Asset Ownership:** Many enslaved individuals were denied the right to own property, accumulate assets, or inherit wealth. Calculations may include the value of property and assets that could have been passed down through generations.

6. **Contemporary Economic Disparities:** Reparations should account for the contemporary economic disparities that disproportionately affect Black communities in the Americas and other parts of the world. This includes wage gaps, disparities in homeownership, and inequalities in access to education and healthcare.

TRANSATLANTIC REPARATION PAYMENTS

This unfathomable suffering befell an estimated 19 million individuals over four centuries, encompassing those Africans forcibly transported to the Americas and Caribbean and those born into slavery.

The Brattle Report, is a groundbreaking report on Reparations for Transatlantic Chattel Slavery in

the Americas and the Caribbean. This report strives to reshape the discourse surrounding one of humanity's darkest chapters: the transatlantic slave trade. The report underscores several harms that defy economic quantification. Given the profound and enduring nature of this harm, the total harm estimated from enslavement falls within the range of US$100 trillion to US$131 trillion for both the harms inflicted during the period of slavery and those that persisted thereafter.

The report also delivers the startling revelation that Britain alone owes an astounding £18.6 trillion for its role in this grievous episode.

The report categorize the harm into two distinct temporal phases: harm during the era of chattel slavery and ongoing harm thereafter.,

FIGURE 1: SUMMARY OF QUANTIFICATION FOR THE ENSLAVEMENT PERIOD

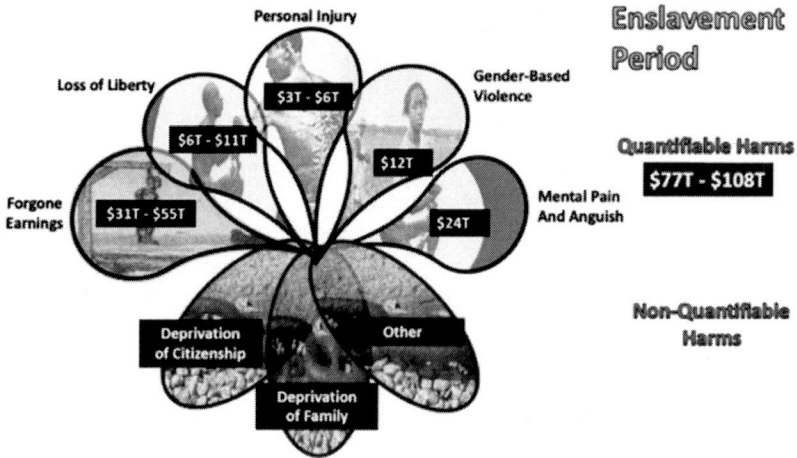

Summary of Quantification for the Enslavement Period Source : The Brattle Report

For the period of enslavement, which includes any post-emancipation "apprenticeship" period where the formerly enslaved ostensibly earned their freedom, reparations are estimated to range between US$77 trillion and US$108 trillion. The lower-bound estimate of US$77 trillion employs an alternative approach that brings the value of stolen labour forward to the present and uses an interest rate grounded in the appreciation of labour's value rather than an interest rate tied to the appreciation of currency's value.

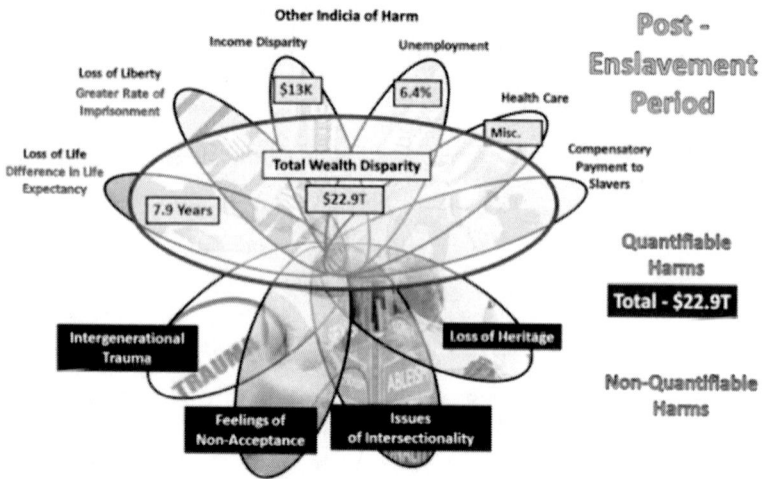

Summary of Quantification for the Enslavement Period Source : The Brattle Report

Turning to the post-enslavement period, various sources of harm come to the fore. These include the loss of liberty, manifested in the over-incarceration of Afro-descendants, income disparities, unemployment, lack of access to healthcare, compensatory payments made by the enslaved to slave owners, and other persistent harms stemming from institutionalized racism. These ongoing injustices encompass political disenfranchisement, physical safety concerns, and, in many nations, underdeveloped economic prospects and resilience.

Taken together, the total harm estimated from enslavement falls within the range of US$100 trillion to US$131 trillion; this recognizes the fact that these figures likely underestimate the true scope of harm.

The report delves into the multifaceted aftermath of slavery, calculating the true cost, encompassing not only economic losses but also the intangible costs. It meticulously examines the recognition of intergenerational trauma, loss of heritage, and the resulting disparities in life expectancy, employment opportunities, and income.

One of the report's standout aspects is its quantification of cumulative wealth and GDP amassed by nations that exploited African labour, highlighting the systemic enrichment of European countries and revealing a web of culpability extending beyond individual actions. Equally noteworthy is the report's analysis of both the enslavement and post-enslavement eras. The figure of £103 trillion, which exceeds the 2019 collective GDP of the entire world, underscores the magnitude of this historical injustice.

The report also brings attention to the disconcerting fact that £20 million was paid to British enslavers in 1833, an amount equivalent to £17 billion today. Astonishingly, British taxpayers, including descendants of the enslaved, such as the Windrush generation, continued to bear the burden of this compensation, obtained through a Bank of England loan, until 2015. This unbroken financial thread highlights the enduring ties that bind the present to a past in dire need of reconciliation.

In conclusion, the lack of reparations for transatlantic slavery is a profound injustice that continues to cast a long shadow over the descendants of enslaved Africans. It is a moral imperative that transcends time, rooted in the principles of justice, human rights, and historical responsibility. Addressing this historical wrong through reparations is not only a matter of acknowledging the past but also a crucial step toward building a more just and equitable future for all. It is a recognition of the enduring legacy of slavery and the moral duty to rectify the injustices it has left in its wake.

REPARATIONS FOR THE COLONIZATION OF AFRICA BY EUROPEAN POWERS

The question of reparations for the colonization of Africa by European powers is a complex and contentious issue that has garnered international attention and debate. Colonization, which spanned several centuries and resulted in significant socio-economic, political, and cultural disruptions, left a lasting impact on the African continent. Here is an examination of the arguments for and against reparations for colonization:

Arguments for Reparations

Colonial-era activity was morally wrong and indefensible: European colonial powers, through their aggressive conquests and exploitation of African resources, bear historical responsibility for the suffering and injustices inflicted on African nations and peoples. Colonising countries justified their actions on the basis of cultural and racial superiority. This ethnocentric approach over-valued western traditions and undervalued those of the countries which were colonised. They undermined the property and social rights of the countries that were colonised and also promoted the success of military might in ordering world affairs over more peaceful resolution. These are all core elements of a colonial mind-set. They are not simply a by-product of colonialism, but rather they form part of the very nature of colonial thinking. They are completely out of step with what is now regarded as appropriate or desirable behaviour in world affairs, indigenous property, and social rights. Reparations would provide a meaningful act of apology for such wrongs.

Reparations would represent an important demonstration of the healing of colonial scars. Many of the problems that now face former colonies can be traced in part or in whole to the actions of colonial-era masters (e. g. the ethnic tensions in Rwanda and Burundi). To move on from the damaging legacy of that era, it is therefore necessary for former colonial powers to make some tangible show that they have closed the colonial chapter of their history and they are seeking a new, more co-operative relationship with developing countries which were their former colonies. It is also important to demonstrate that they now recognise the needs of former colonies rather than simply exploiting the economic opportunities offered by them. In this way, reparations would be an effective way of demonstrating a coming together across the ages.

There are precedents for paying reparations to states or peoples in compensation for historical wrongs. Germany pays an annual amount to Israel and Japan paid reparations after World War II to former colonial possessions such as Korea. More recently, Britain has paid some compensation to the Maoris of New Zealand for damage done in colonial times, and the USA has similarly compensated Native American tribes for broken treaties. Iraq pays compensation to Kuwait for damage done during its invasion and occupation of 1990-91. Why shouldn't former colonies in Africa be similarly trusted to use reparations money wisely?

One suggestion for Africa has been that reparations should pay for free universal education. Another is that proper North-South and East-West railway links be constructed to improve trade within Africa.

Reparations would be an effective way of righting the economic imbalance caused by colonialism. Much of the justification for colonialism, although it may have been given other excuses, was that it was essentially economic in nature. It concerned colonising countries who identified countries with rich natural resources or human resources, and little ability to defend themselves. They would then seek to colonise such countries as a way of providing natural resources and sometimes cheap labour for their own markets as well as possible a market for their goods. Given that colonial powers such as Britain and France gained much of their present prosperity in this way, and that colonised countries continue to suffer economically from the legacy of colonialism, it is both appropriate and logical that the economic imbalance ought to be corrected. As the word "reparations" suggests, this is exactly what reparations would do – they would rebalance the economic relationship between the two countries in a way that sought to correct the historical wrongs.

Reparations represent a concern for the developing world independently of colonial-era wrongs. Even alongside all of the colonialism-based arguments for reparations, we might argue that there are strong other justifications for reparations. The developed world in many cases recognises the dire poverty and social challenges faced by the developing world today. Yet simply giving aid as an act of charity can be embarrassing and demeaning, both for the donor and the recipient in different ways. A system of reparation can facilitate the same partial transfer of wealth from developed world to developing world, but in a way which is more sensitive to these concerns. It allows aid to be given to the developing world in a way which is dignified but not spurious.

Jamaica is seeking $10.6 billion — the equivalent to the fees that Britain paid slave owners to populate the island. One lawmaker has said, arguing that Britain owes those slaves' descendants, at a minimum, their ancestors' purchase price.

Burundi has demanded $43 billion from Germany and Belgium, a figure it says is calculated from the economic toll of decades of forced labor and colonialist violence.

Germany committed $1.35 billion in aid to Namibia alongside a formal acknowledgment of Germany's colonial-era genocide there. Germany's apology was carefully hedged, seemingly to avoid creating precedent that could potentially apply to other colonial abuses, much less to the act of colonization itself.

Under growing pressure, France repatriated 26 pilfered artworks to Benin last year. A French government audit estimated that the country's museums hold 90,000 objects looted from Africa alone, making the return of 26 items like an insult.

In conclusion, the question of reparations for colonization is a deeply contentious one that continues to be a subject of debate and discussion. While there are compelling arguments for acknowledging historical injustices and addressing their consequences, practical challenges, complexities, and differing viewpoints make it a difficult issue to resolve definitively. Ultimately, any efforts to address the legacies of colonization should involve a combination of strategies, including acknowledging history, promoting economic development, and supporting social and cultural preservation, while also respecting the sovereignty and agency of African nations in determining their own futures.

CHAPTER 15
THE AFRICAN QUEST FOR LIBERATION AND INDEPENDENCE

THE AFRICAN QUEST FOR LIBERATION, independence, and nation-building is a complex and inspiring story of resilience and determination. This section explores the historical struggles for freedom, the movements for independence from colonial rule, and the challenges faced in the ongoing process of post-colonial nation-building across the African continent.

This section explores the early forms of resistance to colonialism and highlights the bravery and resilience of those who defied oppressive colonial powers.

Indigenous Defenders and Adaptations: Indigenous peoples often possessed intricate knowledge of their lands which they used to their advantage. Guerrilla warfare, ambushes, and hit-and-run tactics were employed by indigenous warriors to resist colonial forces.

Many indigenous communities also adapted to the presence of colonizers through trade alliances, cultural exchange, and the selective adoption of new technologies.

Rebellion and Uprisings: Armed uprisings were common forms of resistance against colonial rule. For example, the Zulu War in southern Africa, led by leaders like Shaka Zulu, Mau Mau uprising, Yaa Asantewaa I, the Queen of the Ashanti Empire, King Jaja of Opobo, the Oba of Benin, Koitalel Arap Samoei of Kenya, displayed indigenous military prowess.

Cultural Preservation: Resistance to colonialism often took the form of preserving cultural traditions, languages, and belief systems. Indigenous communities sought to safeguard their identities in the face of cultural assimilation.

Indigenous oral traditions, storytelling, and the transmission of knowledge through generations played a vital role in preserving cultural heritage.

Diplomacy and Negotiation: Some indigenous leaders engaged in diplomatic efforts to protect their communities. Treaties and negotiations were pursued to maintain autonomy and secure favourable terms with colonial authorities.

Diplomatic resistance often involved indigenous leaders advocating for the recognition of their sovereignty and rights.

Revolt and Independence Movements: Over time, resistance to colonial rule evolved into movements for national independence. Leaders like Kwame Nkrumah in Ghana championed nonviolent resistance and civil disobedience.

The struggle for self-determination, often marked by protests, strikes, and boycotts, ultimately led to the dismantling of colonial empires.

Legacy and Lessons: Early resistance to colonialism paved the way for future struggles for independence and self-determination. It highlighted the power of unity, determination, and resilience in the face of oppression.

The legacy of these early resistance efforts continues to inspire modern movements for justice, human rights, and decolonization worldwide.

Pan-Africanism: The Pan-African movement, championed by figures like W.E.B. Du Bois and Marcus Garvey, advocated for the unity and liberation of African peoples worldwide. Pan-Africanism sowed the seeds for future independence movements and solidarity.

GHANA'S PATH TO INDEPENDENCE

During World War II , the Gold Coast Regiment sent 65,000 troops to fight for Britain; at least 15,000 lost their lives in battle. The Gold Coast Regiment had fought for Britain in East Africa, Burma and the Gambia. Many believed that the service of people from the Gold Coast during the war negotiated with the British government that Ghana be granted independence after the war. This seemed even more likely because countries that had been allies of Britain during World War II , such as the USA and the Soviet Union, supported giving British colonies their independence after the war.

At the end of World War II in 1945, the troops from the Gold Coast Regiment returned to the Gold Coast, now known as Ghana, after fighting for Britain. However, the Gold Coast did not get its independence. Instead, soldiers returned to the Gold Coast to high levels of unemployment and increased taxes.

In 1947, the United Gold Coast Convention party (UGCC) was set up by a group known as the Big Six. This was the first political party formed by the local people within the colony, and it was a significant step towards self-government. One of the key figures in Ghana's struggle for independence was Kwame Nkrumah, who became the leader of the country's independence movement in the early 1950s.

By 1948, British rule made people in the Gold Coast Colony increasingly frustrated. Of the 54,000 Gold Coast Regiment troops returning home from World War II , more than 53,000 were still unemployed. On February 28, 1948, a group of unarmed former soldiers joined to protest peacefully. They asked the governor of the Gold Coast for the payment they had been promised for their contribution to the war. The British officials stopped the protesters and fired openly into the crowd. Three veterans were killed instantly: Sergeant Adjetey, Corporal Attipoe and Private Odartey Lamptey.

Riots broke out immediately and the UGCC demanded that the British set up a new government led by Africans if they wanted to stop the riots. The riots continued for another five days, shops and stores were looted, and more deaths occurred. The riots ended with the arrest of the UGCC leaders and the British introducing the new Riot Act.

The Accra riots marked a turning point in the independence struggle as they brought the issue of Ghana's independence to the forefront of the international stage. The British were also under pressure from international allies such as the USA, so they were forced to allow this political party to form peacefully.

By 1949, Nkrumah founded the Convention People's Party (CPP), which became the dominant political force in Ghana. Nkrumah's famous slogan was, "Seek ye first the political kingdom and all other things shall be added unto you." This became the rallying cry of Ghana's independence movement.

In 1951 the British government agreed to hold national elections on the Gold Coast. Negotiations with the British government followed, and on March 6, 1957, Ghana became the first sub-Saharan African country to gain independence, with Nkrumah as its Prime Minister. Ghanaian Independence Day has been cele-brated on March 6 every year since.

The 1950s and 1960s witnessed a wave of decolonization across Africa as countries gained independence from their colonial rulers.

CHALLENGES OF POST-COLONIAL NATION-BUILDING:

The borders of contemporary African nations are largely the result of colonial powers dividing the continent among themselves in the late 19th and early 20th centuries. These arbitrary boundaries often cut across ethnic, cultural, and linguistic lines, creating challenges for governance, identity, and stability in post-colonial Africa. This section explores the complexities and challenges posed by post-colonial borders and ethnic diversity on the African continent.

1. **Ethnically Diverse Nations:** Africa is incredibly ethnically diverse with thousands of distinct ethnic groups and languages. In many cases, the borders of post-colonial nations do not align with these ethnic divisions, leading to challenges in nation-building and governance.

2. **Ethnic Conflicts:** Ethnic tensions and conflicts have been a recurring issue in many African countries. Competition for resources, political power, and historical grievances have fuelled ethnic violence and civil wars.

3. **Identity and Belonging:** Individuals and communities often identify strongly with their ethnic or tribal heritage, sometimes more so than with the nation-state to which they belong. This sometimes leads to a sense of dual identity and divided loyalties.

4. **Political Marginalization**: Ethnic minorities often face political marginalization, with power concentrated in the hands of the dominant ethnic group. This result in unequal access to resources and opportunities.

5. **Economic Disparities:** Ethnic disparities in access to education, healthcare, and economic opportunities persist in many African nations and contribute to social and economic inequality.

6. **Displacement and Refugees:** Ethnic conflicts and political instability have led to the displacement of millions of

Africans, resulting in refugee crises within and beyond the continent's borders.

7. **Governance Challenges:** Governing ethnically diverse nations can be challenging. Leaders must balance the interests of various ethnic groups, which can lead to political instability and gridlock.

8. **Nationalism vs. Ethnic Identity:** The promotion of national unity and identity can sometimes conflict with the preservation of ethnic identity. Striking a balance between these competing forces is a complex task.

9. **Border Disputes:** Disputes over borders, particularly in regions with mixed ethnic populations, have led to tensions and conflicts between neighbouring nations.

10. **Regional Organizations and Solutions:** - Regional organizations like the African Union (AU) and the Economic Community of West African States (ECOWAS) have sought to address some of these challenges by promoting regional integration and conflict resolution.

In conclusion, the challenges posed by post-colonial borders and ethnic diversity in Africa are complex and multifaceted. While these issues have contributed to conflicts and governance challenges, they also reflect the richness and diversity of African cultures and traditions. Addressing these challenges requires inclusive governance, respect for ethnic diversity, and efforts to promote economic and social equality. Ultimately, African nations must find ways to harness the strength of their diversity while working towards a more harmonious and stable future.

ECONOMIC DEPENDENCY:

The legacy of colonialism continues to exert a significant impact on the economic structures of many African nations. Post-colonial economic dependency, characterized by reliance on former colonial powers and global economic systems, poses several challenges to the development and self-sufficiency of African economies. This section examines the challenges associated with post-colonial economic dependency in Africa and explores potential solutions.

1. **Limited Economic Diversification:** Many African economies remain heavily dependent on a few primary commodities, such as oil, minerals, or agricultural products. This lack of diversification makes these economies vulnerable to fluctuations in global commodity prices.

2. **Neo-Colonialism:** Neo-colonialism refers to the continued economic dominance and exploitation of former colonies by former colonial powers and other global actors. This manifest through unequal trade relationships, debt burdens, and foreign influence in domestic policies.

3. **Debt Burden:** African nations often carry substantial external debt, much of which originated during the colonial era. Servicing these debts diverts resources away from essential social and economic development programs.

4. **Trade Imbalances:** African countries often face trade imbalances with exports of raw materials exceeding imports of finished goods. This trade structure perpetuates dependency and hinders industrialization.

5. **Unequal Access to Global Markets:** African nations encounter trade barriers, including tariffs and non-tariff barriers, when attempting to access global markets. These barriers limit the growth of domestic industries and exports.

6. **Limited Infrastructure Development**: The focus on extracting and exporting raw materials has sometimes resulted in inadequate investment in infrastructure, hindering economic diversification and competitiveness.

7. **Brain Drain:** Skilled Africans often seek opportunities abroad due to limited prospects at home. This brain drain deprives African nations of valuable human capital.

8. **Aid Dependency:** While foreign aid can be crucial for addressing immediate humanitarian needs, long-term dependency on aid can undermine economic self-sufficiency and sovereignty.

9. **Corruption and Governance Issues:** Corruption and governance challenges further exacerbate economic dependency by diverting resources away from productive sectors and discouraging foreign investment.

10. **Lack of Technological Advancement:** Insufficient investment in research, development, and technology has hindered African countries' ability to compete in global markets and innovate.

Potential Solutions:

Diversification: African nations should diversify their economies by investing in sectors beyond commodities, such as manufacturing, technology, and services.

Regional Integration: Promoting regional economic integration can enhance intra-African trade and reduce dependence on external markets.

Debt Relief: Advocating for debt relief and responsible lending practices can alleviate the burden of external debt.

Investment in Education: Investing in education and skills development can help retain human capital and foster innovation.

Good Governance: Addressing corruption and improving governance is essential for creating an environment conducive to economic growth and investment.

In conclusion, the challenges of post-colonial economic dependency in Africa are formidable but not insurmountable. African nations must pursue policies that promote economic diversification, reduce debt burdens, and foster good governance. Regional cooperation and global partnerships that prioritize mutual benefits rather than exploitation can also play a significant role in helping African economies achieve greater self-sufficiency and prosperity.

POLITICAL INSTABILITY:

Political instability and governance challenges, including corruption and authoritarianism, plague several African nations.

Political instability has been a recurring challenge in many African nations since gaining independence from colonial rule. This instability manifests in various forms, including coups, civil conflicts, and governance crises, and hinders socio-economic development and democratic progress. This section explores the challenges associated with post-colonial political instability in Africa and examines potential solutions to address this pressing issue.

Leadership Challenges: African nations have experienced a range of leadership challenges, including authoritarian rule, corruption, and the entrenchment of ruling elites. These issues erode trust in government institutions and hinder political stability.

Ethnic and Tribal Tensions: Ethnic and tribal divisions, often exacerbated by colonial legacies, have contributed to conflicts and instability in many African countries. Political leaders sometimes exploit these divisions for personal gain.

Weak Democratic Institutions: Weak democratic institutions, such as electoral bodies and judicial systems, can result in contested elections, disputes, and political crises. This undermines the credibility of democratic processes.

Economic Disparities: Economic inequalities, coupled with high levels of poverty and unemployment, can fuel social unrest and political instability as marginalized populations seek change through protests and demonstrations.

Foreign Interference: External actors, including former colonial powers and global powers, sometimes interfere in African politics by supporting certain leaders or factions for their own interests. This can exacerbate conflicts and instability.

Security Challenges: Security threats, such as terrorism and insurgency, can destabilize governments and regions, leading to protracted conflicts and displacement.

Youth Unemployment: High levels of youth unemployment can create a disaffected and politically volatile demographic that is susceptible to radicalization and involvement in protests or violence.

Potential Solutions:

Good Governance: Strengthening governance institutions, enhancing transparency, and combating corruption are essential for building stable political systems.

Conflict Resolution: Addressing ethnic and tribal tensions requires inclusive dialogue, reconciliation processes, and efforts to promote social cohesion.

Economic Development: Fostering economic growth and reducing inequalities can mitigate the socio-economic drivers of political instability.

Democratic Consolidation: Strengthening democratic institutions, ensuring free and fair elections, and upholding the rule of law are critical for democratic consolidation.

Peacebuilding: International and regional organizations can play a vital role in supporting peacebuilding efforts and conflict resolution.

In conclusion, the challenges of post-colonial political instability in Africa are complex and multifaceted and rooted in historical, social, and economic factors. Addressing these challenges requires a comprehensive approach that encompasses governance reform, conflict resolution, economic development, and regional cooperation. By working collectively to strengthen institutions, promote inclusivity, and prioritize the welfare of their citizens, African nations can chart a path towards greater political stability and sustainable development.

THE ROLE OF AFRICAN UNITY:

African unity, a vision long held by African leaders and intellectuals, plays a pivotal role in addressing the continent's complex challenges. Since the era of decolonization, African nations have recognized the need to foster unity among diverse countries and cultures. This section explores the multifaceted role of African unity in addressing continent-wide challenges, from political and economic stability to social and cultural collaboration.

1. Political Stability and Conflict Resolution: African unity through regional organizations like the African Union (AU) facilitates conflict prevention and resolution. Collective diplomatic efforts can help mitigate intra-state and inter-state conflicts.

Peacekeeping: Joint peacekeeping missions and interventions are made more effective when African nations cooperate. For instance, the AU has deployed peacekeeping forces to conflict zones to promote stability.

2. Economic Development and Integration:

Intra-Africa Trade: African unity promotes intra-Africa trade by reducing trade barriers and facilitating the movement of goods and services across borders. Initiatives like the African Continental Free Trade Area (AfCFTA) aim to boost economic growth.

Resource Utilization: Collective resource management and investment in regional infrastructure projects are made possible through unity. Joint efforts can harness Africa's vast resources for sustainable development.

3. Health and Pandemic Response:

Disease Control: Unity enables coordinated responses to health crises like Ebola and, more recently, the COVID-19 pandemic. African nations can pool resources for healthcare infrastructure and vaccine distribution.

Health Research: Collaborative research and development efforts within the African scientific community contribute to better healthcare outcomes.

4. Education and Cultural Exchange:

Educational Partnerships: African unity fosters educational partnerships among nations, enabling the exchange of knowledge and expertise.

Cultural Promotion: Collective efforts to preserve and promote African culture strengthen the cultural identity and provide opportunities for cultural exchange and collaboration.

5. Environmental Conservation:

Environmental Protection: Africa faces environmental challenges, including climate change and wildlife conservation. Unity enables coordinated efforts to protect the continent's natural heritage and address environmental threats.

6. Human Rights and Social Justice:

Advocacy: African unity amplifies the continent's voice on global human rights issues and allows for collective advocacy.

Solidarity: When faced with social justice challenges, such as xenophobia or discrimination, African nations can demonstrate solidarity and support for affected communities.

7. Infrastructure Development:

Transportation: Joint infrastructure projects, like trans-African highways and railways, enhance connectivity and promote economic growth.

Energy: Collaboration on energy projects, such as the Grand Inga Dam, can address energy shortages and promote industrialization.

8. International Diplomacy:

Negotiation Power: African unity strengthens the continent's position in international negotiations on issues like trade, climate, and peace.

Representation: United, African nations can advocate for reforms in global institutions to ensure fair representation.

In conclusion, African unity is not merely an ideal; it is a pragmatic approach to addressing the continent's complex challenges. Through political, economic, and social collaboration, African nations can leverage their collective strength to overcome obstacles and seize opportunities. By fostering unity, African nations work toward a future of stability, prosperity, and shared progress for the benefit of all Africans.

Contemporary Challenges and Opportunities:

Youth Empowerment: Africa's youth demographic presents both opportunities and challenges for the continent's future. Efforts to empower youth through education, employment, and civic engagement are central to sustainable development.

Infrastructure and Development: Infrastructure development, including transportation, energy, and healthcare, is essential for African nations to achieve economic growth. International partnerships and investments play a role in advancing these objectives.

In conclusion: The African quest for liberation, independence, and post-colonial nation-building is an epic tale of resilience, courage, and the pursuit of self-determination. Despite the enduring challenges, including political instability, economic dependency, and ethnic diversity, African nations have made remarkable progress.

African unity, regional cooperation, and the engagement of youth hold promise for a brighter future. The legacy of the struggle for independence and the ongoing quest for development underscore the importance of recognizing Africa's historical journey and supporting its continued efforts for progress, stability, and self-realization.

THE ROLE OF INTERNATIONAL PARTNERSHIPS IN FOSTERING AFRICAN DEVELOPMENT

International partnerships play a vital role in advancing Africa's development agenda. Africa, a continent with diverse challenges and opportunities, benefits from collaboration with foreign governments, international organizations, and non-governmental entities. This section explores the multifaceted role of international partnerships in fostering African development, addressing key areas where collaboration is crucial.

1. Economic Development and Investment:

Foreign Direct Investment (FDI): International partnerships attract FDIs, which stimulate economic growth, infrastructure development, and job creation. Partnerships can facilitate favourable investment environments.

Development Assistance: Bilateral and multilateral development assistance provides financial and technical support for vital sectors like healthcare, education, and agriculture.

2. Trade and Market Access:

Trade Agreements: Bilateral and regional trade agreements provide African nations with access to international markets. These agreements can boost exports and diversify economies.

Market Access: International partnerships often come with preferential market access, benefiting African goods and services.

3. Infrastructure and Connectivity:

Infrastructure Financing: Partnerships can fund critical infrastructure projects, including transportation, energy, and telecommunications, which are essential for economic development.

Connectivity: Collaboration on transcontinental transportation networks and digital infrastructure enhances connectivity within Africa and with the global economy.

4. Health and Education:

Healthcare Initiatives: International partnerships support healthcare systems, disease control, and pandemic response. They can also facilitate access to vaccines and medical supplies.

Education Programs: Collaborative efforts improve educational access, quality, and curriculum development. Scholarships and exchange programs broaden opportunities for African students.

5. Technology and Innovation:

Technology Transfer: Partnerships promote technology transfer and knowledge sharing, fostering innovation and competitiveness in African industries.

Research Collaboration: Joint research projects and academic partnerships contribute to advancements in science and technology.

6. Peace and Security:

Conflict Resolution: International partnerships aid in conflict prevention, peacekeeping, and post-conflict reconstruction efforts.

Counterterrorism: Collaboration on counterterrorism initiatives enhances security in regions affected by extremist groups.

7. Environmental Sustainability:

Climate Initiatives: International cooperation on climate change mitigation and adaptation supports Africa's resilience to environmental challenges.

Conservation: Conservation partnerships protect Africa's biodiversity and natural resources.

8. Governance and Capacity Building:

Institutional Strengthening: Partnerships promote good governance, rule of law, and capacity building in government institutions.

Election Monitoring: International organizations assist in ensuring free and fair elections, promoting democratic processes.

9. Humanitarian Assistance:

Humanitarian Aid: International partnerships provide crucial humanitarian aid during crises, including food aid, shelter, and medical support.

Refugee Assistance: Collaboration supports refugees and displaced populations and addresses displacement challenges.

In conclusion, international partnerships are indispensable in advancing African development goals and overcoming the continent's complex challenges. These partnerships leverage resources, expertise, and global influence to drive economic growth, improve healthcare and education, enhance infrastructure, and promote peace and security. African nations must continue to engage in strategic collaborations to unlock their full potential and achieve sustainable development for their people.

CHAPTER 16
THE BUILDING OF ISRAEL

THE ESTABLISHMENT of the State of Israel in 1948 was a momentous event in the history of the Jewish people and the culmination of decades of political, social, and ideological efforts. This chapter examines the multifaceted journey of building the modern State of Israel, encompassing the early Zionist movement, the struggle for independence, and the subsequent challenges and achievements that have shaped this vibrant nation.

1. The Roots of Zionism: The Zionist movement, initiated in the late 19th century, sought to address the challenges facing Jewish communities around the world. Prominent figures like Theodor Herzl and Chaim Weizmann advocated for the establishment of a Jewish homeland in historic Palestine.

The publication of Herzl's "The Jewish State" in 1896 laid the intellectual groundwork for the Zionist endeavor.

2. Balfour Declaration and British Mandate: The Balfour Declaration of 1917, issued by the British government, expressed support for the establishment of a "national home for the Jewish people" in Palestine.

Following World War I, the League of Nations granted Britain a mandate over Palestine and Jewish immigration into the region increased significantly.

3. Struggle for Independence: Tensions between Jewish immigrants and Arab Palestinians escalated over time, leading to conflicts and violence. Jewish paramilitary organizations like the Haganah and Irgun played pivotal roles in the struggle for independence.

The United Nations' 1947 partition plan, which recommended the establishment of separate Jewish and Arab states in Palestine, was a critical step towards Israel's creation.

The period leading up to the declaration of the State of Israel was marked by intensified clashes between Jewish paramilitary groups and Arab forces. These confrontations included the King David Hotel bombing in 1946 by the Irgun, which killed 91 people, and the Deir Yassin massacre in 1948, in which over 100 Palestinian villagers were killed.

The United Nations Special Committee on Palestine (UNSCOP) was formed in 1947 to investigate the situation in Palestine and recommend a solution. UNSCOP's majority report recommended partitioning Palestine into separate Jewish and Arab states with international administration for Jerusalem while the minority report proposed a federal state. The majority plan, known as the partition plan, was adopted by the United Nations General Assembly on November 29, 1947.

4. Declaration of the State of Israel:

On May 14, 1948, David Ben-Gurion, Israel's first Prime Minister, proclaimed the establishment of the State of Israel in Tel Aviv. This declaration marked the end of British rule in Palestine, which formally expired at midnight.

Ben-Gurion's proclamation emphasized the historical connection of the Jewish people to the land of Israel and expressed a commitment to equality and democratic principles. He also extended a hand in peace to neighboring Arab states.

The declaration, however, immediately led to conflict as neighboring Arab states, including Egypt, Jordan, Syria, and Iraq, launched military operations in response. The 1948 Arab-Israeli War, also known as the War of Independence, ensued.

The 1948 Arab-Israeli War:

The 1948 Arab-Israeli War was a complex and brutal conflict that lasted until 1949. It involved not only the newly declared State of Israel and its Arab neighbors but also Palestinian Arab militias.

Despite facing military challenges from multiple fronts, Israel managed to secure its existence and expand its territorial control. Armistice agreements were eventually reached with Egypt, Jordan, Syria, and Lebanon, resulting in de facto borders.

CHALLENGES AND ACHIEVEMENTS:

The establishment of the State of Israel in 1948 marked the realization of a long-held dream for the Jewish people. However, the new nation faced a multitude of challenges in its early years. This section explores the significant challenges Israel confronted and the remarkable achievements it accomplished in the decades following its independence.

1. Absorption of Mass Jewish Immigration

Challenge: Israel absorbed waves of Jewish immigrants from Europe, the Middle East, and North Africa. These immigrants came with diverse cultural backgrounds, languages, and needs, placing immense strain on the young nation's resources.

Achievement: Israel successfully integrated millions of immigrants into its society through programs such as absorption centers, Hebrew language courses, and vocational training. This diversity enriched Israeli culture and contributed to its resilience.

2. Security and Defense:

Challenge: Israel faced existential threats from neighboring Arab states and militant groups. The 1948 Arab-Israeli War, the Suez Crisis of 1956, and the Six-Day War in 1967 were just a few of the conflicts that tested Israel's security.

Achievement: Israel developed a robust defense apparatus, including the Israel Defense Forces (IDF), to protect its borders and citizens. The country's military innovations, including its intelligence agencies and advanced weaponry, bolstered its security.

3. Nation-Building and Economic Development:

Challenge: Building a functioning government, infrastructure, and economy from scratch was a monumental task. Israel had to secure its financial stability and provide for a growing population.

Achievement: Israel's emphasis on education, research, and technology led to remarkable economic growth. The "Start-Up Nation" became renowned for its high-tech industry, agricultural advancements, and innovative solutions to water scarcity.

4. Diplomacy and Peace Efforts:

Challenge: Israel's relationship with its Arab neighbors remained fraught with tensions and conflicts. Achieving lasting peace in the region seemed elusive.

Achievement: Israel engaged in diplomatic efforts and signed peace agreements with Egypt in 1979 and Jordan in 1994. While the Israeli-Palestinian conflict persists, there have been periods of negotiation and efforts to find a peaceful resolution.

5. Social and Cultural Integration:

Challenge: Israel's diverse population included Jews from various cultural backgrounds as well as Arab citizens and other minorities. Fostering a sense of national identity and cohesion was essential.

Achievement: Israel's cultural mosaic reflects the rich tapestry of Jewish heritage and a vibrant democracy. Hebrew, the national language, became a unifying force, and cultural expression flourished in art, literature, and music.

6. Technological Advancements:

Challenge: Israel's small size and limited natural resources compelled it to invest heavily in innovation and technology to ensure its economic viability.

Achievement: Israel's technological advancements have had a global impact. The country is a leader in fields like cybersecurity, agriculture, medical research, and renewable energy.

7. Humanitarian Aid and International Cooperation:

Challenge: Israel faced criticism and diplomatic challenges due to the Israeli-Palestinian conflict and regional tensions.

Achievement: Despite these challenges, Israel has contributed to international humanitarian efforts, including disaster relief, medical assistance, and technological cooperation, earning respect on the global stage.

In conclusion, the challenges faced by Israel following its independence were immense, but the nation's resilience, innovation, and commitment to democratic values have resulted in remarkable achievements. Israel's ability to overcome adversity and thrive in various fields has made it a dynamic and influential nation in the global community. As it continues to navigate complex geopolitical challenges, its achievements serve as a testament to the indomitable spirit of a nation born from a dream.

SIMILARITIES BETWEEN THE ESTABLISHMENT OF ISRAEL AND AFRICAN STATES

The establishment of the State of Israel and the struggle for independence of African nations were significant historical events that unfolded in the mid-20th century. While these events occurred in vastly different regions with distinct contexts, there are notable similarities in the challenges and processes involved in nation-building. This section explores these commonalities, shedding light on the shared experiences of statehood.

1. **Struggles Against Colonialism:** Similarity: Both Israel and many African states were emerging from colonial rule. Israel faced British control in Palestine while African nations were liberating themselves from European colonial powers, such as Britain, France, and Belgium.

Shared Challenge: The struggle for independence and the assertion of sovereignty were common goals, motivating both Israelis and Africans to resist colonial domination.

2. **Diversity of Populations:** Similarity: Israel and numerous African nations are characterized by diverse populations with people from various ethnic, cultural, and religious backgrounds.

Shared Challenge: Building a cohesive national identity while respecting and accommodating this diversity was a challenge. Efforts to forge unity and inclusivity were central to nation-building.

3. **Absorption of Mass Migration:** Similarity: Israel absorbed millions of Jewish immigrants from around the world while African states received returning diaspora communities and refugees displaced by colonialism.

Shared Challenge: The absorption of large numbers of people with varying backgrounds and needs placed significant strain on resources and infrastructure. Accommodating these populations and fostering a sense of belonging were key challenges.

4. Security Concerns:

Similarity: Both Israel and newly independent African states faced security challenges, including border disputes, regional conflicts, and the need to establish military capabilities.

Shared Challenge: Ensuring the security of their borders and populations was a top priority for both Israel and African nations, leading to the development of military forces and defense strategies.

5. Economic Development:

Similarity: Israel and African states sought economic development to secure their independence and improve the living standards of their populations.

Shared Challenge: The task of building a functioning economy, infrastructure, and institutions was a common challenge. Efforts were made to promote agriculture, industry, and trade.

6. Diplomatic and International Relations:

Similarity: Israel and African states engaged in diplomacy and sought international recognition and support for their sovereignty.

Shared Challenge: Gaining recognition on the global stage and navigating complex international relations required diplomatic efforts and alliances.

7. Nation-Building and Identity:

Similarity: Both Israel and African states grappled with the complex task of nation-building, fostering a sense of identity, and instilling a shared national narrative.

Shared Challenge: Establishing institutions, education systems, and cultural expressions that could unite diverse populations was crucial to creating a sense of belonging.

8. Legacy of Independence:

Similarity: The struggles for independence in Israel and African states left lasting legacies and shaped the national identities, values, and aspirations of their respective populations.

Shared Achievement: These nations celebrated their independence as a testament to the determination and resilience of their people, forging unique national identities.

In conclusion, despite the geographical and historical differences between the establishment of Israel and the independence movements in African states, there are notable similarities in the challenges faced and the processes involved in nation-building. These shared experiences highlight the universal aspirations for self-determination, sovereignty, and the pursuit of a better future that transcended borders and continents during the mid-20th century.

COMPARING ZIONISM AND PAN-AFRICANISM

Zionism and Pan-Africanism are two influential political and social movements that emerged in the late 19th and early 20th centuries. While they have distinct historical contexts and objectives, they share common elements related to the pursuit of self-determination, identity, and empowerment for their respective communities. This section provides a comparative analysis of Zionism and Pan-Africanism, exploring their origins, ideologies, goals, and impacts.

Zionism: Zionism emerged in the late 19th century as a political and ideological movement among Jewish communities in response to anti-Semitism and discrimination in Europe. It was influenced by Jewish thinkers like Theodor Herzl, who advocated for the establishment of a Jewish homeland in historic Palestine.

Zionism is based on the belief in Jewish self-determination and the establishment of a Jewish state in Eretz Yisrael (Land of Israel). It emphasizes the importance of preserving Jewish culture, religion, and identity through the establishment of a Jewish homeland.

The primary goal of Zionism was realized with the establishment of the State of Israel in 1948. Israel serves as a homeland and refuge for Jews from around the world, offering a place where Jewish culture, religion, and identity can flourish.

Zionism has had a profound impact on Jewish identity and history. It led to the establishment of Israel as a vibrant and diverse nation-state with a significant Jewish population. It also sparked complex geopolitical dynamics in the Middle East.

Pan-Africanism: Pan-Africanism emerged in the late 19th and early 20th centuries as a response to colonialism, racism, and the exploitation of African nations and peoples. Figures like W.E.B. Du Bois and Marcus Garvey played pivotal roles in shaping the movement.

Pan-Africanism is rooted in the belief in the unity and solidarity of people of African descent worldwide. It advocates for the eradication of colonialism, racism, and discrimination, and the promotion of African culture and self-reliance.

The primary goal of Pan-Africanism is the liberation and empowerment of African nations and the promotion of African unity. It has led to the formation of organizations like the African Union and efforts to promote economic development and political cooperation among African countries.

Pan-Africanism has had a significant impact on the decolonization process in Africa and the formation of independent African nations. It continues to influence African politics, culture, and international relations.

Comparative Analysis:

1. **Identity and Self-Determination:** Both Zionism and Pan-Africanism emphasize the importance of identity, self-determination, and empowerment for their respective communities. They seek to address historical injustices and create spaces where their cultures and identities can flourish.

2. **Responses to Oppression:** Both movements emerged as responses to oppression, discrimination, and marginalization. Zionism responded to anti-Semitism in Europe while Pan-Africanism responded to colonialism and racism in Africa and the African diaspora.

3. **Formation of Nations:** Zionism led to the formation of the State of Israel while Pan-Africanism played a role in the decolonization of African nations and the establishment of independent African states.

4. **International Impact:** Both movements have had international repercussions. Zionism has influenced the geopolitics of the Middle East while Pan-Africanism has shaped African politics, diplomacy, and international relations.

5. **Cultural Preservation:** Both movements emphasize the preservation and promotion of their respective cultures, languages, and traditions as integral components of their identities.

Differences between Zionism and Pan-Africanism:

1. **Geographic Focus:** One of the primary differences between the two movements is their geographic focus. Zionism is primarily concerned with the establishment and preservation of a Jewish homeland in the historic Land of Israel whereas Pan-Africanism has a global scope, seeking to unite people of African descent worldwide,

including those in Africa, the Americas, and the
Caribbean.

2. **Historical Context:** Zionism emerged in response to anti-
   Semitic persecution in Europe and the desire for a Jewish
   homeland. In contrast, Pan-Africanism developed as a
   response to colonialism, racism, and the exploitation of
   African nations during the colonial era.

3. **Religious vs. Cultural Emphasis**: Zionism has a strong
   religious and historical dimension, emphasizing the
   significance of the Land of Israel in Jewish history and
   culture. In contrast, Pan-Africanism places greater
   emphasis on cultural unity and solidarity among people of
   African descent, irrespective of religious differences.

4. **Political Structures:** Zionism led to the establishment of a
   nation-state, Israel, with its own government and political
   institutions. Pan-Africanism, on the other hand, is more of
   a political and cultural movement that has influenced the
   politics and diplomacy of multiple African nations and the
   African Union but has not resulted in a single united
   African state.

5. **Responses to Historical Wrongs:** While both movements
   are responses to historical injustices, they address different
   forms of oppression. Zionism seeks to address centuries of
   anti-Semitic persecution, including the Holocaust, and the
   need for a Jewish homeland. Pan-Africanism addresses the
   legacy of colonialism, the transatlantic slave trade, and
   systemic racism.

6. **International Relationships:** Zionism has complex
   relationships with neighboring countries and international
   actors, particularly in the Middle East. Pan-Africanism has
   focused on fostering cooperation and solidarity among
   African nations and the African diaspora, often in the
   context of international organizations.

In conclusion, Zionism and Pan-Africanism, while sharing some common themes of identity, self-determination, and empowerment, are distinct movements with unique historical contexts, ideologies, and objectives. Zionism led to the establishment of a nation-state, Israel, while Pan-Africanism has influenced the decolonization process and political cooperation in Africa. Both movements have had profound impacts on their respective communities and have contributed to global discussions on identity, self-determination, and justice. Understanding these differences and similarities is essential for appreciating their significance in the broader context of social and political movements.

CHAPTER 17
INTERSECTIONS BETWEEN JEWISH AND AFRICAN DIASPORA EXPERIENCES

THE HISTORIES of Jewish and African diaspora communities are characterized by displacement, discrimination, and resilience. This section explores the intersections between these two distinct yet interconnected experiences, highlighting instances of collaboration and solidarity in their shared struggles against discrimination and oppression.

Historical Parallelism:

Dispersal and Displacement: Both Jewish and African diaspora communities experienced forced dispersal and displacement from their ancestral lands. The Jewish diaspora dates to antiquity while the African diaspora was further complicated by the transatlantic slave trade and other historical migrations.

Persecution and Discrimination: Throughout history, both communities have faced persecution, discrimination, and marginalization. Jewish communities encountered discrimination in Europe while African diaspora communities endured slavery, colonialism, and apartheid.

Shared Experiences of Discrimination:

Anti-Semitism and Racism: Anti-Semitism and racism are deeply ingrained forms of discrimination that both communities have grappled with.

Racial profiling, stereotypes, and systemic oppression have been common experiences.

Economic Exploitation: Both Jewish and African diaspora communities have faced economic exploitation, from the ghettoization of Jewish populations to forced labour and exploitation in colonial settings.

Economic inequality and lack of access to opportunities persist in various contexts.

Instances of Collaboration and Solidarity:

Civil Rights Movement in the United States: The American Civil Rights Movement was a pivotal moment of collaboration between Jewish and African American communities.

Jewish individuals, inspired by their own history of oppression, played key roles in supporting civil rights leaders like Dr. Martin Luther King Jr.

Anti-Apartheid Struggle in South Africa: Jewish communities around the world actively supported the anti-apartheid movement in South Africa.

Organizations like the American Jewish Committee and individuals like Joe Slovo were instrumental in advocating for justice and equality.

Cultural Exchange and Mutual Influences:

Cultural Contributions: Jewish and African diaspora communities have enriched the world with their cultural contributions. The fusion of Jewish klezmer music with African rhythms, for instance, exemplifies the creative intersections of these cultures.

Literature and Art: Jewish and African diaspora writers and artists have explored themes of identity, displacement, and discrimination in their works.

Authors like Toni Morrison and Isaac Bashevis Singer have left lasting legacies in the world of literature.

Shared Values and Lessons:

The Pursuit of Justice: Both communities share a commitment to justice, equality, and human rights.

The Jewish concept of "Tikkun Olam" (repairing the world) aligns with the African diaspora's pursuit of social justice.

Resilience and Survival: The shared experiences of resilience and survival in the face of adversity are powerful lessons.

Both communities draw strength from their histories to confront contemporary challenges.

In conclusion, the intersections between Jewish and African diaspora experiences reveal a complex tapestry of shared struggles, collaboration, and solidarity. While each community's journey is distinct, their historical parallels and common commitment to justice and equality have created opportunities for collaboration and mutual support.

These intersections serve as a reminder of the enduring human spirit and the potential for positive change when diverse communities come together to confront discrimination and oppression. The lessons learned from these collaborations emphasize the importance of empathy, solidarity, and the shared pursuit of a more just and inclusive world.

LEARNING FROM ISRAEL

Israel, a nation established in the mid-20th century, has made remarkable strides in various fields, transforming itself into a modern and developed state. African nations, with their unique challenges and opportunities, can draw valuable lessons from Israel's journey. This section explores key areas in which African nations can learn from Israel's experiences and achievements.

1. Innovation and Technology: Israel's focus on innovation and technology has made it a global leader in fields such as cybersecurity, agriculture, and medical research. African nations can learn to prioritize investments in research and development, foster entrepreneurship, and leverage technology for economic growth and development.

Developing a robust tech ecosystem, supporting startups, and creating innovation hubs can spur economic diversification and job creation.

2. Education and Human Capital: Israel places a high value on education, boasting a well-developed education system from primary to tertiary levels. African nations can learn the importance of investing in human capital through quality education.

Emphasizing STEM (Science, Technology, Engineering, and Mathematics) education can equip African youth with the skills needed for a knowledge-based economy.

3. Water Resource Management: Israel's expertise in water resource management, including desalination and irrigation technologies, can provide crucial lessons for water-scarce regions in Africa.

Implementing efficient water management practices can enhance food security, promote agriculture, and address water shortages.

4. Agriculture and Food Security: Israel's advancements in agriculture, particularly in arid and semi-arid regions, offer insights for African nations struggling with food security.

African countries can adopt drip irrigation, precision agriculture, and crop breeding techniques to improve agricultural productivity and ensure food self-sufficiency.

5. Diaspora Engagement: Israel's successful engagement with its global diaspora, including financial and intellectual contributions, can serve as a model for African nations in harnessing the potential of their diaspora communities.

Encouraging diaspora investments and knowledge transfer can boost economic development and create connections with global markets.

6. Defense and Security: Israel's experience in ensuring its security and defense in a volatile region can inform African nations facing security challenges.

Collaboration on regional security issues, intelligence sharing, and capacity-building can help stabilize conflict-prone areas.

7. Economic Diversification: Israel's commitment to diversifying its economy, moving beyond traditional sectors, can inspire African nations to explore new industries and reduce reliance on a single economic driver.

Promoting sectors like tourism, renewable energy, and manufacturing can contribute to economic resilience.

8. Innovation Ecosystems: Israel's vibrant innovation ecosystems, characterized by cooperation between academia, government, and the private sector, can be emulated by African nations.

Developing research and innovation centers, providing incentives for private sector R&D, and fostering partnerships between universities and industries can stimulate innovation.

Encouraging diaspora investments and knowledge transfer can boost economic development and create connections with global markets.

In conclusion, Israel's journey from its inception to a modern and developed state offers valuable lessons for African nations. By prioritizing innovation, education, sustainable resource management, and economic diversification, African countries can make significant progress toward building prosperous and modern states. Learning from Israel's experiences can inspire African nations to tackle their unique challenges and realize their full potential on the global stage.

LESSONS FROM JEWISH DESERT FARMING

The arid landscapes of Israel, particularly the Negev Desert, have seen remarkable transformations through innovative agricultural practices pioneered by Jewish farmers. These practices offer valuable lessons for agricultural development in Africa, a continent that grapples with food security challenges and increasing aridity due to climate change. This section explores key insights from Jewish desert farming that can benefit agricultural endeavours in Africa.

1. Drip Irrigation Technology:

Jewish farmers in Israel have perfected the use of drip irrigation, a water-efficient method that delivers small, consistent amounts of water directly to plant roots. This technology minimizes water wastage, making it possible to cultivate crops in water-scarce regions. African nations facing water scarcity can adopt and adapt drip irrigation to optimize water use and ensure crop survival in dry spells.

2. Soil Improvement Techniques:

Desert farming demands the enhancement of soil quality. Jewish farmers have employed techniques like composting, mulching, and the addition of organic matter to improve soil fertility. African countries should prioritize soil health through sustainable practices to boost crop yields and ensure long-term agricultural viability.

3. Crop Selection and Adaptation:

Jewish farmers have chosen crops that thrive in arid conditions, such as date palms, pomegranates, and drought-resistant varieties of grains. African nations should prioritize research and cultivation of crops suitable for their specific climates and water availability, thereby increasing resilience against changing weather patterns.

4. Agroforestry and Shade Agriculture:

The practice of agroforestry, integrating trees and crops, provides shade, reduces evaporation, and improves soil quality. African farmers can adopt similar strategies to enhance crop resilience and protect against soil degradation.

5. Community Collaboration:

Jewish desert farming often involves communal efforts with farmers sharing knowledge and resources. African communities can benefit from collaborative farming practices that promote knowledge sharing, access to resources, and collective problem-solving.

6. Research and Innovation:

Investment in agricultural research and innovation is crucial for adapting to changing conditions. Israel's commitment to research and development has led to the creation of arid-resistant crop varieties and improved farming techniques. African nations should allocate resources to agricultural research to address specific challenges and foster innovation.

7. Sustainable Practices:

Jewish desert farming prioritizes sustainable practices to ensure long-term viability. Techniques like organic farming, minimal tillage, and crop rotation can reduce environmental degradation and improve soil health.

Jewish desert farming showcases the transformative potential of innovative agricultural practices in arid environments. As Africa grapples with increasing aridity and food security challenges, adopting and adapting these lessons can lead to more resilient, sustainable, and productive agriculture. By embracing technologies, sustainable practices, and community collaboration, African nations can harness their agricultural potential to ensure food security, economic growth, and improved livelihoods for their citizens.

LEARNING FROM JEWISH ENTREPRENEURSHIP AND INNOVATION

Entrepreneurship and innovation have been key drivers of economic growth and prosperity in many communities around the world, including the Jewish community. Jewish entrepreneurship, with its emphasis on creativity, resilience, and adaptability, offers valuable lessons for Black Africa, a region with immense untapped potential. In this section, we will explore what Black Africa can learn from Jewish entrepreneurship and innovation.

1. Value of Education:

Jewish culture places a strong emphasis on education, which has contributed to a highly skilled and educated workforce. Black Africa can benefit from investing in education and vocational training to develop a skilled labour force that can drive innovation and entrepreneurship.

2. Resilience and Adaptability:

Jewish history is marked by resilience in the face of adversity. Despite facing numerous challenges, Jewish entrepreneurs have demonstrated a remarkable ability to adapt to changing circumstances. Black African entrepreneurs can draw inspiration from this resilience and develop the ability to pivot and innovate when faced with obstacles.

3. Global Networks:

The Jewish diaspora has created extensive global networks, facilitating international trade and collaboration. African entrepreneurs can leverage their diaspora communities to expand their businesses and access international markets, fostering economic growth.

4. Innovation Ecosystems:

Israel, often dubbed the "Startup Nation," has created a thriving innovation ecosystem that encourages entrepreneurship and fosters creativity. African nations can learn from Israel's success by investing in infrastructure, providing access to capital, and creating supportive regulatory environments for startups and innovation hubs.

5. Philanthropy and Mentorship:

Jewish tradition places a strong emphasis on philanthropy and giving back to the community. Successful Jewish entrepreneurs often serve as mentors and investors in startups. Encouraging a culture of philanthropy and mentorship can help nurture the next generation of African entrepreneurs.

6. Risk-Taking:

Entrepreneurship often involves taking calculated risks. Jewish entrepreneurs have a reputation for taking bold risks that lead to innovation and growth. African entrepreneurs can learn the importance of calculated risk-taking in seizing opportunities and driving progress.

7. Leveraging Technology:

Israel has excelled in the technology sector, particularly in fields like cybersecurity, agriculture technology, and medical research. African nations can invest in technology-driven industries and leverage innovation to address local challenges and create global solutions.

8. Government Support:

Israel's government has played a role in supporting entrepreneurship through grants, incentives, and policy frameworks. African governments can learn from Israel's approach by creating an enabling environment for startups and small businesses.

9. Collaboration and Partnerships:

Jewish entrepreneurs often collaborate and form partnerships with other businesses and research institutions. African entrepreneurs can seek opportunities for collaboration, both within the continent and with global partners, to access resources, markets, and expertise.

Jewish entrepreneurship and innovation provide a powerful model for Black Africa to follow as it seeks to unlock its economic potential. By prioritizing education, resilience, diversity, mentorship, and innovation, African nations can cultivate a new generation of entrepreneurs who drive economic growth, create jobs, and address the unique challenges facing the continent. Through these efforts, Africa can harness its entrepreneurial spirit to build a brighter, more prosperous future for its people.

LEARNING FROM AFRICAN CULTURAL DIVERSITY AND UNITY

Jewish culture and history have much to gain from the cultural diversity and unity found within Black African societies. Inclusivity and hospitality are two fundamental aspects of Black African culture that carry valuable lessons for the Jewish community. While both communities have their unique histories and traditions, there is much to be gained from understanding and adopting these principles. Here are several key lessons that Jews can learn:

1. **Celebration of Diversity:** Black Africa is incredibly diverse with thousands of ethnic groups and languages. Yet, despite this diversity, many African societies have found ways to celebrate and appreciate the unique contributions of each group. Jews can learn to celebrate the diversity within their own community and appreciate the richness it brings.

2. **Community and Family Bonds:** Traditionally African societies frequently place a strong emphasis on community and family values. These close-knit relationships provide vital social support networks. Jews can reflect on the importance of community and family in their own lives and traditions.

3. **Welcoming the Stranger:** A central tenet of Black African culture is the warm welcome extended to strangers and guests. The concept of "ubuntu" in some African societies emphasizes the interconnectedness of all people and encourages a sense of communal responsibility. Jews can draw from this by fostering a culture of welcoming newcomers, immigrants, and visitors with open arms. Embracing strangers enriches the community and promotes a sense of unity.

4. **Breaking Down Barriers:** In many African cultures, there are fewer formal barriers between individuals. Social

hierarchies are often less rigid, allowing for greater interaction and connection among people from different backgrounds. Jews can learn to break down barriers within their own community and beyond and thereby promote inclusivity and unity among diverse groups.

5. **Acts of Kindness (Tzedakah)**: While the Jewish tradition highly values acts of charity (tzedakah), Black African cultures often emphasize communal support and helping those in need. Black African communities often extend hospitality and support to people from diverse backgrounds, including refugees and immigrants. Jews can learn to expand their acts of kindness and generosity, both within their community and by extending assistance to those outside it, fostering a sense of collective responsibility for the welfare of all.

6. **Bridging Divides**: In many African societies, there is a strong tradition of conflict resolution and reconciliation. Mediation and dialogue are used to bridge divides and heal wounds. Jews can apply this approach to address internal divisions or conflicts and work towards reconciliation and unity.

7. **Celebration of Music and Dance**: African cultures celebrate life through music and dance. Jews can embrace the joy of music and dance as forms of expression and celebration within their own traditions. While both cultures have their unique musical traditions, there are important insights to be gained from the African approach to music and dance. African societies often use music and dance as expressions of joy, celebration, and communal bonding. Jews can learn to infuse their own celebrations and rituals with the exuberance and emotional depth that music and dance can bring.

African music and dance often have deep spiritual significance and connect individuals with their beliefs and spirituality. It has the power to bridge cultural divides, foster understanding among diverse groups and often has a global appeal. By learning from the celebration of music and dance in Black African culture, the Jewish community can enhance its own cultural richness, sense of community, and share their own musical traditions with a wider global audience, promoting cross-cultural understanding.

Incorporating the principles of inclusivity and hospitality from Black African culture into the Jewish community can lead to a more open, welcoming, and compassionate society. By embracing these values, transcending geographical boundaries, Jews can contribute to fostering a spirit of unity, understanding, and shared humanity in an increasingly diverse world.

LEARNING FROM AFRICAN SUSTAINABLE LIVING PRACTICES

Black African societies have a rich history of sustainable living practices that can offer valuable insights to the Jewish community and the world as a whole. These practices, rooted in harmony with nature and resourcefulness, provide lessons that can be applied to modern Jewish life.

1. **Environmental Stewardship:** African cultures often have a deep respect for nature and the environment. Sustainable farming methods, such as agroforestry and crop rotation, have been passed down through generations. The Jewish community can embrace a greater sense of environmental stewardship by adopting eco-friendly practices, promoting conservation, and reducing waste.

2. **Self-Reliance and Community Cooperation:** African societies often rely on community cooperation for survival. Neighbours share resources and labour, strengthening social bonds and promoting self-reliance. Jewish communities can explore the benefits of self-

reliance and cooperative efforts, especially in times of need.

3. **Sustainable Agriculture:** Sustainable farming practices in Africa, such as terracing and rainwater harvesting, are designed to ensure food security without depleting natural resources. These methods can inspire Jewish communities to adopt more sustainable approaches to food production and distribution.

4. **Preservation of Traditional Knowledge:** African cultures have preserved traditional knowledge related to sustainable living for generations. This includes indigenous farming techniques, herbal medicine, and water management systems. Jews can similarly value and preserve traditional knowledge and thus ensure that ancient wisdom is not lost to time.

5. **Adaptability and Resilience:** African societies have shown remarkable adaptability and resilience in the face of adversity. Jews can learn to navigate challenges with greater flexibility and resilience by drawing from the strength of their history and traditions.

6. **Circular Economies:** African communities often practice circular economies, where waste is minimized and resources are reused and recycled. Jews can explore ways to reduce waste and embrace more sustainable consumption patterns.

7. **Harmonious Living with Wildlife:** In many African cultures, there is a tradition of coexisting peacefully with wildlife. This respect for the natural world can inspire Jews to consider their own relationship with animals and the environment.

8. **Traditional Medicine and Healing Practices:** African cultures have a rich tradition of herbal medicine and natural healing practices. Jewish communities can explore complementary and alternative medicine approaches that prioritize holistic well-being.

9. **Community Resilience in Times of Crisis:** African communities often come together to support one another during times of crisis, whether it's famine, conflict, or natural disasters. Jewish communities can strengthen their own sense of unity and support networks to navigate challenges effectively.

By embracing these sustainable living practices and lessons from Black African culture, the Jewish community can contribute to a more environmentally conscious, resilient, and harmonious way of life. These shared values of sustainability and resourcefulness can foster greater understanding and cooperation between the two communities.

LESSONS FOR TODAY'S GLOBAL STRUGGLES:

A. Intersectionality: The Civil Rights Movement highlighted the importance of intersectionality by recognizing that social justice movements must address various forms of discrimination simultaneously. Contemporary movements for gender equality, and immigrant rights often draw from this intersectional perspective.

B. Grassroots Activism: Grassroots activism played a central role in the Civil Rights Movement's success. Today's global movements, including environmental activism and social justice campaigns, emphasize the power of grassroots mobilization.

The Role of Youth:

Youth-Led Movements: The Civil Rights Movement was significantly influenced by young activists and students. Youth-led movements today, such as the climate strikes and youth participation in political activism, continue this tradition of driving social change.

The Intersection of Generations: The passing down of knowledge and activism from one generation to the next is a vital aspect of the Civil Rights Movement's legacy.

Interactions between older activists and youth today contribute to the ongoing fight for justice.

Global Responses to Injustice:

International Solidarity: The Civil Rights Movement demonstrated the power of international solidarity in advancing the fight against racial discrimination. Global expressions of support, such as protests and boycotts, played a role in pressuring the U.S. government to enact change.

Challenges Beyond Borders: The global fight against racial discrimination faces complex challenges, including systemic racism, economic inequality, and political disenfranchisement.

International cooperation and advocacy remain essential in addressing these issues.

Acknowledging the Universal Nature of Displacement:

Lesson from History: The Jewish and African diasporas exemplify the universal nature of displacement. They teach us that migration and forced exile are not isolated events but part of a broader human experience.

Contemporary Implication: Recognizing this universality encourages us to approach contemporary migration with empathy and compassion. It reminds us that displacement can happen to anyone, regardless of their background.

Providing Safe Havens and Asylum:

Lesson from History: Both diasporas have experienced the dire consequences of being denied safe havens and asylum. The tragic consequences of such denial are evident in events like the Holocaust and the horrors of the transatlantic slave trade.

Contemporary Implication: Learning from these historical tragedies, we must advocate for robust asylum systems that prioritize human rights and provide refuge to those fleeing violence, persecution, and natural disasters.

Addressing Root Causes:

Lesson from History: The historical narratives in this book highlight the importance of addressing root causes of displacement, whether it's religious persecution, political instability, or economic hardships.

Contemporary Implication: Our approach to contemporary migration and refugee issues must extend beyond humanitarian aid to address the systemic causes of displacement. This involves diplomacy, conflict resolution, and efforts to reduce poverty and inequality.

Embracing Cultural Diversity:

Lesson from History: The Jewish and African diasporas demonstrate the resilience of cultural identities in the face of migration. They've preserved their languages, traditions, and customs.

Contemporary Implication: In receiving communities, an appreciation for cultural diversity is essential. Efforts should be made to create inclusive societies that embrace the richness brought by newcomers while ensuring their cultural preservation.

Building Empathy and Solidarity:

Lesson from History: Both diasporas have faced discrimination and prejudice throughout their histories. Their stories underscore the importance of empathy and solidarity.

Contemporary Implication: We must actively combat discrimination, xenophobia, and racism in our societies. Emphasizing shared values and shared humanity can foster greater empathy and solidarity toward migrants and refugees.

Global Cooperation:

Lesson from History: The historical movements of these diasporas occurred within a global context. The Holocaust, for instance, was a global tragedy.

Contemporary Implication: Our approach to migration and refugees must involve international cooperation. Global challenges require global solutions and collaboration among nations is paramount in addressing displacement effectively.

The Role of Education:

Holocaust and Slavery Education: Holocaust education and education about the history of slavery are essential tools for understanding and empathy. They promote awareness of the consequences of discrimination and oppression.

Promoting Empathy: Education programs that encourage empathy and intercultural understanding are vital. These programs foster a sense of shared humanity and a commitment to justice.

A Shared Journey:

A Vision for the Future: The Jewish and African diaspora communities share a vision of a more inclusive, equitable world. Their stories serve as a call to action for addressing discrimination, promoting unity, and advancing empathy.

B. The Legacy of Collaboration: The enduring legacy of collaboration between these communities will continue to inspire future generations. It serves as a testament to the potential for positive global change when diverse communities come together.

In conclusion, the enduring legacies of the Jewish and African diasporas are a testament to the resilience, creativity, and unwavering commitment to justice and equality of these communities.

As they navigate ongoing challenges, they serve as a source of inspiration for the world.

Their stories remind us that, regardless of the difficulties faced, the human spirit can triumph over adversity. Through unity, empathy, and the shared pursuit of a more inclusive and just world, the enduring legacies of these diaspora communities offer a vision of hope and a call to action for all of humanity. In their shared journey, we find a path towards a brighter, more equitable future.

In conclusion, the comparative history of the Jewish and African diasporas serves as a powerful reminder that our approach to contemporary migration and refugee issues should be rooted in empathy, human rights, and a deep understanding of the complex factors driving displacement. These historical narratives challenge us to build inclusive, compassionate, and just societies, where the shadows of suffering are replaced by the light of hope and humanity. By applying the lessons from this history, we can work toward a world where all individuals, regardless of their origin, can find safety, dignity, and opportunity.

CONCLUSION

Throughout this book, we have journeyed through the intricate histories of two remarkable diaspora communities—the Jewish and African diasporas. We have traced their origins, witnessed their struggles, celebrated their resilience, and examined their enduring legacies. As we conclude this exploration, it's crucial to reflect on the broader significance and contemporary relevance of comparative diaspora history.

Understanding Humanity's Shared Experiences:

Connecting the Dots: Comparative diaspora history illuminates the interconnectedness of human experiences. It reminds us that, regardless of our cultural or ethnic backgrounds, we share a common history of migration, displacement, and adaptation.

Empathy and Solidarity: Learning about the trials and triumphs of different diaspora communities fosters empathy and solidarity. It encourages us to stand together against discrimination, prejudice, and injustice.

Challenging Preconceptions and Stereotypes:

Breaking Stereotypes: Comparative history challenges stereotypes and misconceptions. It dismantles narrow views of diaspora communities and exposes the rich tapestry of their experiences.

Cultural Diversity: By examining multiple diasporas, we appreciate the diversity within and between communities. We understand that no single narrative defines any group.

Navigating Contemporary Issues:

Migration and Refugees: Comparative diaspora history informs our approach to contemporary migration and refugee issues. It highlights the urgency of addressing displacement and providing safe havens for those in need.

Identity and Belonging: As we grapple with questions of identity and belonging in today's globalized world, the stories of diaspora communities offer valuable insights into the complexities of identity formation and cultural preservation.

Lessons in Resilience and Adaptation:

Resilience: Both Jewish and African diasporas have demonstrated remarkable resilience in the face of adversity. Their stories inspire us to persevere in times of challenge.

Adaptation: Adaptation and cultural preservation are central themes in diaspora history. They teach us the importance of preserving cultural heritage while embracing change.

Building Bridges and Fostering Dialogue:

Cross-Cultural Understanding: Comparative diaspora history fosters cross-cultural understanding and dialogue. It encourages us to engage in meaningful conversations about our shared past and future.

Promoting Peace: Understanding the historical roots of conflicts, such as the Israeli-Palestinian conflict or the legacy of colonialism in Africa, can contribute to peaceful resolution and reconciliation.

Charting a Path Forward:

Social Justice: The lessons from diaspora histories inform our commitment to social justice and equity. They remind us of the importance of combating discrimination and marginalization.

Global Citizenship: Comparative diaspora history invites us to become global citizens and be aware of the interconnectedness of our world and our shared responsibility to create a more inclusive and compassionate future.

As we conclude our journey through the Jewish and African diasporas, we recognize that comparative diaspora history is not merely a study of the past; it is a roadmap for the future. It empowers us to shape a world where diversity is celebrated, where the lessons of history guide our actions, and where the shadows of suffering give way to the light of understanding, unity, and justice. This book is a testament to the enduring strength of diaspora communities and an invitation to all of us to be stewards of a more inclusive and compassionate world.

The importance of remembering and learning from history cannot be overstated in our quest to build a more inclusive and compassionate world. History, as our collective memory, serves as a beacon of guidance and a source of profound wisdom. It offers us valuable lessons about empathy, justice, and the significance of diversity, while also cautioning us against the perils of discrimination, conflict, and oppression.

As we reflect on the enduring legacies of our past, we recognize that history empowers us to be better individuals and global citizens. It challenges us to confront and rectify past mistakes, to embrace the beauty of our diverse world, and to champion the values of compassion and inclusivity.

Remembering and learning from history is not a passive act but a call to action. It compels us to be agents of positive change in our communities and beyond. It encourages us to promote empathy, tolerance, and justice in our daily lives and to support social justice movements that seek a fairer and more equitable world.

Ultimately, the lessons of history point us toward a brighter future, one where the collective wisdom of our past shapes our present actions. By doing so, we can construct a world where inclusivity and compassion are not mere ideals but the very foundations upon which our societies are built. It is a vision that is not only attainable but one that is essential for the well-being and progress of humanity.

GLOSSARY

Advocacy: The act of actively supporting a cause, policy, or group and working to promote its interests or goals.

Apartheid: A system of institutionalized racial segregation and discrimination that was enforced in South Africa from 1948 to 1994.

Archives: Collections of historical documents, records, and materials that are preserved for research and reference purposes.

Collective Memory: The shared recollection of events, experiences, and cultural knowledge within a society or community.

Chattel Slavery: A form of slavery where individuals are considered property and are bought, sold, and owned for life.

Civil Rights Movement: A social and political movement in the United States that sought to end racial segregation and discrimination against African Americans and promote their civil rights.

Critical Thinking: The ability to think logically, analyse information, and evaluate arguments and evidence objectively.

Cultural Exchange: The sharing of cultural practices, ideas, and traditions between different groups or communities.

Cultural Preservation: Efforts to protect and maintain the traditions, languages, customs, and heritage of a particular culture or community.

Diaspora: The dispersion or scattering of a people from their original homeland, often used to describe communities living outside their ancestral lands.

Discrimination: Unfair treatment or prejudice against individuals or groups based on characteristics such as race, ethnicity, gender, religion, or nationality.

Empathy: The capacity to understand and share the feelings and perspectives of others.

Genocide: The intentional and systematic extermination of a national, ethnic, racial, or religious group.

Global Citizenship: A sense of belonging to a broader global community and a commitment to addressing global issues and challenges.

Globalization: The process of increased interconnectedness and interdependence among countries and cultures, often driven by advances in technology and trade.

Global Issues: Challenges or problems that transcend national boundaries and require international cooperation and solutions, such as climate change, poverty, and human rights violations.

Historical Trauma: Psychological and emotional wounds that are passed down through generations as a result of collective experiences of violence, oppression, or injustice.

Holocaust: The systematic genocide of six million Jews and millions of others by Nazi Germany during World War II.

Inclusivity: The practice or policy of including people from diverse backgrounds and perspectives, ensuring that everyone feels welcome and valued.

Intercommunity Collaboration: Cooperation and partnership between different communities, often with the goal of addressing shared challenges or advancing common values.

Intercommunity Engagement: Active involvement and interaction between different communities or groups, often for the purpose of building understanding and cooperation.

Memorials: Physical structures, monuments, or sites created to honour and remember significant historical events, figures, or tragedies.

Oral Tradition: The transmission of knowledge, stories, and cultural practices through spoken language rather than through written records.

Pan-Africanism: A movement that advocates for the unity and cooperation of African and African diaspora communities world-wide with a focus on addressing social, political, and economic issues.

Remembrance Days: Special dates and events dedicated to remembering historical events or commemorating the lives and sacrifices of individuals or groups.

Resilience: The ability to withstand and recover from adversity or difficult situations.

Social Justice Movements: Grassroots or organized efforts to address societal inequalities and injustices, often advocating for the rights of marginalized groups.

Social Justice: The fair and equitable distribution of resources, opportunities, and privileges within society, often addressing issues of inequality and discrimination.

Tikkun Olam: A Jewish concept that translates to "repairing the world," emphasizing the responsibility of individuals to work for social justice and improve the world.

Warning Signs: Indicators or signals that suggest potential problems or issues, often used in the context of preventing conflicts or crises.

REFERENCE

"Diaspora Nationalism and Jewish Identity in Habsburg Galicia" by Joshua Shanes:

"Diaspora and Zionism in Jewish-American Literature: Lazarus, Syrkin, Reznikoff, and Roth" by Ranen Omer-Sherman:

"Diasporas in the New Media Age: Identity, Politics, and Community" edited by Andoni Alonso and Pedro J. Oiarzabal:

"Diaspora, Politics, and Globalization" edited by Gabriel Sheffer

"Diaspora as Homeland: German-Jewish Writing in the Twentieth Century" by Yasemin Yildiz

"Discovery Of the Oldest Adornments in The World". National Centre for Scientific Research also known as Centre National de La Recherche Scientifique (CNRS). Published by EurekAlert! 18th June, 2007. https://www.eurekalert.org/pub_releases/2007-06/c-dot061807.php

"From Babylon to Timbuktu: A History of the Ancient Black Races Including the Black Hebrews" by Rudolph R. Windsor.

"From Ambivalence to Betrayal: The Left, the Jews, and Israel" by Robert S. Wistrich:

"Human Y chromosome haplogroup R-V88: a paternal genetic record of early mid Holocene trans-Saharan connections and the spread of Chadic languages". Cruciani F, Trombetta B, Sellitto D, Massaia A, Destro-Bisol G, Watson E, Beraud Colomb E, Dugoujon JM, Moral P, Scozzari R (July 2010). European Journal of Human Genetics. 18 (7): 800–7. doi:10.1038/ejhg.2009.231. PMC 2987365. PMID 20051990.

"In Search of Jewish Community: Jewish Identities in Germany and Austria, 1918-1933" by Michael Brenner

"Israel and the American Diaspora" by Calvin Goldscheider

"Israel, Diaspora, and the Routes of National Belonging" by Jasmin Habib

"Is Mansa Musa the richest man who ever lived?" Naima Mohamud. (2019) Published by BBC News, 10 Mar https://www.bbc.com/news/world-africa-47379458

"Jewish Diaspora in Latin America" edited by David Sheinin

"Israel and Its Mediterranean Identity" by Eyal Ginio

"Meet Mansa 1 Of Mali – the richest human being in all of history" John Hall (2012). Published by Independent.co.uk,

"Native African medicine with special reference to its practice in the Mano tribe of Liberia" Harley, George (1941). Cambridge, Mass: Harvard University Press. p. 26. ISBN 978-0-674-18304-9. OCLC 598805544.

"Sorghum Domestication and Diversification: A Current Archaeobotanical Perspective". Dorian Q. Fuller, Chris J. Stevens (2016

"The African Diaspora: A History Through Culture" by Patrick Manning

"The African Diaspora in the United States and Europe: The Ghanaian Experience" by Takyiwaa Manuh

"The African Diaspora: Slavery, Modernity, and Globalization" by Isidore Okpewho, Carole Boyce Davies, and Ali A. Mazrui

"The Americanization of the Synagogue, 1820-1870" by Jonathan D. Sarna

"The Black Diaspora: Five Centuries of the Black Experience Outside Africa" edited by Ronald Segal

"The Global Jewish News Source: An Inside View of Israel and the Jewish World" by Dina Gold

"The History of the Jews: A Brief History" by Lawrence Joffe "The Jewish Diaspora: A Brief History" by John M. Efron

"The Israeli Diaspora" by Steven J. Gold

"The Jews of Modern France" by Paula E. Hyman and Frances Malino

"The Jewish Century" by Yuri Slezkine

"The Jews of Arab Lands: A History and Source Book" by Norman A. Stillman

"The Jews of Europe in the Modern Era: A Socio-Historical Outline" by Viktor Karady

"The Jewish Diaspora in Latin America and the Caribbean: Fragments of Memory" edited by Kristin Ruggiero

"The Jews in the Modern World: A History since 1750" by Hilary L. Rubinstein, William D. Rubinstein, and Gavin I. Langmuir:

"The Jewish Diaspora: A Brief Overview" by John M. Efron

"The Jewish Diaspora in the Former Soviet Union: A Comparative Study of Six Cities in Kazakhstan and Israel" by Zvi Gitelman

"The Making of African America: The Four Great Migrations" by Ira Berlin

"Zionism and the Diaspora: A Newcomer among Brothers" by Asher Cohen

"The Zionist Idea: A Historical Analysis and Reader" edited by Arthur Hertzberg

"Who is an African? Identity, Citizenship and the Making of the Africa-Nation", Jideofor Patrick Adibe (2009), Adonis & Abbey Publishers

"Yam: threats to its sustainability in Nigeria", by Chukwu G.O., M.C. Ikwelle (2000CGPRT Centre Newsletter, 17 (2000)

"82,000-year-old Shell beads From North Africa and implications for the origins of modern human behaviour". PNAS June 12, 104 (24) 9964-9969. https://www.pnas.org/content/104/24/9964"Black Europe and the African Diaspora" edited by Darlene Clark Hine, Trica Danielle Keaton, and Stephen Small

https://www.edutopia.org/article/teaching-african-history-and-cultures-across-curriculum

https://www.sciencedaily.com/releases/2007/06/070618091210.htm

https://en.wikipedia.org/wiki/History_of_mathematics#Prehistoric_mathematics ↑

https://en.wikipedia.org/wiki/Ancient_Egyptian_medicine ↑

https://thinkafrica.net/africas-inventions-algorithms/

https://thinkafrica.net/kola-nut-the-untold-african-story-behind-coke-and-pepsi/

https://thinkafrica.net/africa-2000-domesticated-foods/

https://thinkafrica.net/iron-technology/

https://thinkafrica.net/steel-in-africa/

https://thinkafrica.net/food-domestication-of-yam-in-5000-bc-west-africa/

https://thinkafrica.net/sorghum-more-healthy-than-wheat/

https://thinkafrica.net/walls-of-benin/

https://thinkafrica.net/the-kingdom-of-benin-1660-years-from-355-ad-to-present/

https://thinkafrica.net/kingdom-of-aksum/

https://thinkafrica.net/the-ashante-kingdom/

Made in United States
North Haven, CT
30 October 2023

43414432R00122